# Sales Ex Machina

## How Artificial Intelligence is
## Changing the World of Selling

Victor Antonio, BSEE, MBA
James Glenn-Anderson, PhD

D1595899

Published by Sellinger Group

Copyright © 2018 by Victor Antonio

This publication is designed to provide accurate and authoritative information in regard to the subject matter covered. It is sold with the understanding that the publisher is not engaged in rendering legal, accounting, or other professional services. If legal advice or other expert assistance is required, the services of a competent professional should be sought.

This Sellinger Group Publication Edition is published by Victor Antonio of the Sellinger Group.

Contact Information:

PO Box 4342,

Alpharetta, GA 30023

www.SellingerGroup.com

Printed in the United States of America First Printing: January, 2018

Library of Congress Cataloging in Publication Data

Antonio, Victor and Glenn-Anderson, James

Sales Ex Machina, How Artificial Intelligence is Transforming the World of Selling

ISBN 978-0-578-20083-5 (U.S.A.) 1. Business 2. Sales

0 2 0 1 1 8

# Table of Contents

# INTRODUCTION
# Sales Ex Machina

*Machines are getting smarter with each passing week, month, and year. So, where does that leave us? Where is the world of technology taking us, and how is it changing the way we do business and interact with others? What are the unforeseen implications or unintended consequences for selling and business? How much adaptation will be required for a salesperson to remain relevant? What will we have to know to still be of value in our various business pursuits? And most importantly, where do we fit as sales professionals in this artificially intelligent future?*

The world of selling is changing…again! But this time, it's different. We are about to experience the equivalent of a major tectonic shift where the functional plates of sales, marketing, and technology will shear and, in some cases, smash against another.

Functions that were once the domain of salespeople will be transformed, subsumed, or obliterated.

Does that sound too dramatic? It shouldn't! It's begun to happen already, and far too many executives, managers, business owners, and sales professionals are either ignorant of the fact or are simply too busy trying to achieve their revenue quota to even notice what's happening.

I can only imagine that millions of years ago, a dinosaur looked upward and saw a meteor entering the earth's atmosphere, stared at it for a moment, and then turned away without a second thought—never realizing that the meteor was the harbinger of its own extinction and the world from that moment on would be changed forever.

Artificial intelligence (AI) is that meteor. It's that digital anomaly that has entered our ecosystem, and its impact will be felt globally thanks to the help of various enabling technologies along with a global telecommunication infrastructure.

In the computational sciences, we are seeing an exponential growth in processing power that calls into question, nullifies, and otherwise obviates Moore's Law. For those unfamiliar with the term, Moore's Law is an empirical technology growth model first cited by Gordon Moore, co-founder of Fairchild Semiconductor, who predicted a doubling of the number of transistors in integrated circuit chips every 12 to 18 months.

By several more or less reasonable leaps of logic, this model has also been regarded as a harbinger of increased sophistication in technologies dependent on those integrated circuits, such as computers. This model has held approximately true for quite some time, but now with the advent of intelligent systems and allied technologies, there is evidence we're actually beating the prediction.

In any event, with this increase in computational power, we are also seeing an inverse proportional relationship to cost. That is, the machines are getting more powerful AND cheaper.

These new computers have allowed scientists and technologists to create programs exhibiting a combination of complexity, sophistication, and speed exceeding all that has come before. Some have claimed this computational power and sophistication are beginning to mimic and even rival the human brain in the areas of adaptation and creativity. This is certainly true in some respects. The fact is computers are working harder, better, faster, and getting stronger. Daft Punk[1] captured the electronic ethos of AI:

Work it harder
Make it better
Do it faster
Makes us stronger

More than ever
Hour after hour
Work is never over

Add to this exponential growth in processing power a broadband infrastructure that allows any individual to be connected to any other individual or machine, anywhere in the world, and you can begin to get a glimpse of what this means to businesses, to consumers, and more specifically to sales professionals.

---

[1] Daft Punk is an electronic music duo known for their music but more so for wearing helmets and gloves to assume robot personas. One of their most popular songs is "Harder Better Faster Stronger" on the album *Discovery*, released in 2001 under the Virgin label.

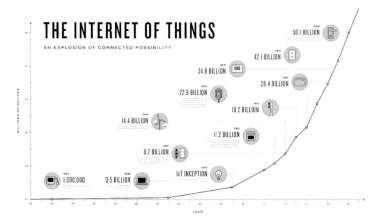

**Figure 1: NCTA.com**

Technology companies have continued to develop systems with the surprising ability to push more and more information through the air (wireless) and glass (fiber optics). Companies are also finding new ways to compress large amounts of data and increase in bandwidth capacity to levels that years ago would've seemed inconceivable. This is all significant and even breathtaking to consider. The term "information superhighway" is beginning to seem like an antiquated analogy; it only references intersystem speed and capacity while ignoring an exponentially increasing trend in embedded machine intelligence.

**GO AI**

In 1997 IBM's computer Deep Blue beat world chess champion Garry Kasparov, leading to the prediction of the rise of AI and how it would soon take over the world. That prediction was a bit premature, but a machine agent beating a human at tactics and strategy? This had previously been considered a domain reserved to humans alone. Thinking people everywhere took note of this development as "handwriting upon the wall."

The question of whether Man or Machine was stronger in terms of brute strength was settled during the Industrial Revolution. Machines were stronger, but still needed humans to operate, design, and maintain. Watching a machine beat a human at strategy and creativity woke the world up to the possibility that our dominance in the realm of intelligence had come to an end. Though a hasty assumption, the coexistence of man and machine has become more and more prominent.

Machines like Deep Blue are programmed with rules that guide its "thinking." So while the machine did win, this victory didn't mean it was necessarily smarter; it could still only perform what was programmed into it. Its "intelligence" did not translate into any other task or process. While impressed with the Deep Blue's performance, we still proclaimed, "It won, but it's still a machine that can only do what we tell it to do; it can't think or learn on its own." We found solace in this little fact and clung to it for reassurance that we hadn't lost our cognitive dominance to a machine.

In March 2016, we saw another milestone in artificial intelligence. An AI computer program called AlphaGo[2] beat South Korean Lee Sedol in a five-game series of Go, a game somewhat akin to chess but, as some have claimed, even more difficult. This was the first time a computer Go program had beaten a 9-dan professional. AlphaGo won the first three games and lost to Sedol in the fourth game. Sedol resigned the final game, giving AlphaGo a 4-1 win. It was the first Computer Go program to beat a human professional Go player.

Just like chess, Go is also a game of strategy, but that's where the direct comparison ends. Go has many more moving

---

[2] AlphaGo is a narrow AI computer program that plays the board game Go. It was developed by Alphabet, Inc.'s Google DeepMind in 2015.

pieces and an incalculable amount of strategic moves and outcomes. An inherent "combinatorial explosion" renders the game much more difficult to master and by default, that more difficult for a machine to master.

Not satisfied with a 4-1 win, the developers improved AlphaGo's algorithm, which had previously used a Monte Carlo algorithm (i.e., one based on statistical trials), to determine what its next move should be. Next they employed a Deep Learning methodology to calculate a next step based on what the program had "learned" from previous moves. In every sense, from philosophical to mathematical to logical, this was much more "up close and personal."

AlphaGo was then ready to take on the next human expert. At the Future of Go Summit in 2017, AlphaGo faced off against Chinese Ke Jie who, at the time, was ranked the No.1 Go player in the world. In a three-game match, AlphaGo won all three!

**The Master Algorithm**
The revelation that a machine algorithm could learn and adapt at a faster pace than humanly possible sparked thinly veiled dire predictions. The machines are getting smarter, begging the question, "Where does that leave us in the world of technology and business?" More to the point, "How much adaptation will be required on the part of a salesperson to remain relevant, and what knowledge or skills will we have to know to still be of value?"

At this juncture, it's worth doing a cursory review of how humans and machines have coexisted to give us some indication of trends, where the relationship might be going.

For the most part, we've used dumb machines like typewriters, printing presses, kitchen tools, and so on by powering them with "muscles" of a sort and straightforward *procedural logic*—"If such-and-such happens, do this-or-that." Thus armed with a touch of electricity and basic functionality, these machines—toasters, calculators, and vacuum cleaners—help us do more with less effort to accomplish a given task.

Next, we added some programmable rules to give the machine more processing power and programs (software) to assist us in generating numerical results more efficiently and accurately, graphics so that we could more easily visualize the process, and a Graphical User Interface (GUI) to facilitate the human-machine interface.

With more processing power came more sophisticated programs, and once users began to realize what might be possible, a vigorous demand cycle quickly ensued (i.e., more processing power triggers development of more sophisticated programs that burden the machine, requiring more processing power and so on).

It was then that we began adding some semblance of intelligence by preloading the machines with a set of "rules" providing answers to simple "What next?" scenarios; think Google Search. In this manner, the user's needs might, to at least some extent, be anticipated. This gives the machine an appearance of being smart.

Well, it is in fact a first step along that path. However, this simple rule-based programming model rapidly reached the end of a useful life cycle. Rule-based programming is in some sense "brittle"; the number of rules is fixed, and the machine is, by virtue of its programming, incapable of adaptively generating new rules to accommodate new situations.

The next step was to get the machine to learn how to think on its own through "supervised learning," whereby some means for providing corrective feedback is added to the mix.

And finally, we are now looking to make the final push into the vast landscape called "unsupervised learning," where the machine begins to learn and adapt (repeat cycle) on its own—so much so that the human programmers don't even know what the algorithms will look like. This is what Pedro Domingos has dubbed The Master Algorithm.[3] In his book of the same name, Domingos discusses the quest of data scientists to build "the ultimate learning machine that will remake our world."

## Deus Ex Machina

The evolution of machines and machine intelligence can be broken down into five epochs:

1. Assist: Hand-powered machines assisted us in leveraging our efforts to do tasks we otherwise would struggle to do with our own strength and effort. Think typewriter, printing press, and so on.

2. Administrate: Computers gave us the power to do knowledge tasks with incredible speed and accuracy. Think proposals, drawings, presentations, and so on.

3. Automate: With some intelligence, the machines were now able to do many of the administrative tasks allowing us to focus on our primary function (job). Think email auto-responders, auto-generated proposals, reports, texts, and so on.

---

[3] Domingos, Pedro. *The Master Algorithm: How the Quest for the Ultimate Learning Machine Will Remake Our World*. Basic Books, 2015.

4. Augment: Intelligent machines can help people find answers faster, retrieve information quickly, and fulfill requests with simple voice or text commands. Think of virtual assistants that can answer questions via text or voice recognition systems that can find the information or content you need.

The fifth and final epoch in the evolution of Machine Learning is Autonomy. Here is where AI begins to blur the lines between human and machine. Here is where the Master Algorithm or the *deus ex machina*[4] comes in to solve the seemingly unsolvable problem of having a machine truly think like a human being.

That said, the goal of this book is not to explore the infinite ways a 5th-level AI machine can change the world, but rather how AI is transforming and will continue to transform the world of selling. With these innovations, or disruptions, come a multitude of questions:

- How will the sales functions be reshaped?
- Who will be impacted?
- How will they be impacted?
- How will the role of sales manager change?
- What tools are (and will be) available?
- How can you use AI to augment the sales process?
- At what point or in which function is having an autonomous AI possible?

---

[4] *Deus ex machina* is Latin and means "god from the machine." Wikipedia offers the following definition: "Over time the term has evolved to mean a plot device whereby a seemingly unsolvable problem is suddenly resolved by the intervention of some new event, character, ability or object. Its function can be to resolve an otherwise irresolvable plot situation, to surprise the audience, [or] to bring the tale to a happy ending."

- What applications are available or will be used?
- How will AI be used to help salespeople sell more?
- How will it help them manage their time?
- How will it help them achieve their revenues with more certainty and speed?

This book is about learning, internalizing, and leveraging AI with respect to sales.

The power of selling is moving away from the individual and toward the machine (*Sales Ex Machina* = Sales from the Machine)—machines that can now prospect, follow-up, present, and propose without human intervention.

In some cases, the machine will obliterate sales functions while in others, it will dramatically shift the locus of focus further into the sales cycle.

To adapt to change, we must first seek to understand it. To adapt to AI, we must first seek to understand its short-term and long-term ambitions and how and where we fit in the new digital ecosystem of selling.

# PART 1: SCIENCE OF AI

# CHAPTER 0

# What Is This AI Thing?

*Like a Rubik's Cube, you turn it this way and that, and nothing seems to work. You keep at it, though, and at some point, you suddenly realize what you're looking at is more than one problem. That is, you see it as composed of pieces, subproblems if you will, which when jointly solved necessarily solve the larger, original problem.*

I'm going to tell a story. You're an up-and-comer in your sales organization. You've done well these past few years—big salary, big commissions, and a very nice office. You're even the boss's favorite, most of the time. Of course, you want to keep what you've won. As a high-performer, you have more responsibility, more products, more customers, and more diverse markets.

You know you're good. Everybody knows it, but this is getting out of hand. The sheer complexity of juggling an ever-increasing body of responsibilities is rapidly becoming overwhelming. For all your excellent work, you're starting to feel insufficient, too small to meet these expectations. What to do?

Now, you happen to have a computer scientist friend. We'll call him Bob. One particular evening, you run into him at a social gathering, and over drinks, you reluctantly let him in on your quandary. You then proceed to explain you don't think you're going to be able to rise further because the complexity of your work has already pushed to your limit and no alternatives seem forthcoming. Your friend is a bit taken aback by this admission as he has never known you to be anything less than completely confident.

Nevertheless, your friend Bob finds this topic interesting. He's become intent, completely focused on what you're saying. Here and there, he interjects some rather pointed questions, all pertaining to the specific problems you face. At some point in your lengthy explanation, he stops you and replies, "What you need is a clone that can work all night!"

You reply, "Yeah, and I want him to work for free!"

You both laugh at this. "Good luck with that!" Bob has grown quiet, seemingly in deep thought. He then looks up and says, "I have an idea."

You reply, "Really?" All the while you're thinking to yourself, "What possible solution could he offer for this mess?!" But you know him; he's sometimes quite clever. He's always thinking at these strange angles. It's that science stuff, of course.

After a moment, he pipes up and says, "I have a different idea. You need an intelligent advisor."

You look at him for a moment, and then reply, "Thanks. You've saved me! I thought you were going to suggest I marry the boss's daughter!" You both laugh at this because your boss only has sons.

"No, no, no… I mean a computer program, one I'll design especially for you—your sales application, that is."

You stare at him for a moment. You reply, "I really don't think a computer program is going to help me. This thing requires 'smarts.'"

Your friend replies, "No, no, no… This is different. This program *will be* smart, just like you. It's called artificial intelligence, 'AI' for short, and it will do all the dumb stuff you do!"

Again, you both start laughing at the quasi-Freudian, backhanded compliment. You remain disbelieving of course, but still somewhat intrigued. "You're serious?!"

Bob looks at you, totally serious now. "Yes. It's a well-established technology, and I think it can help you."

Now, you're incredulous. "What is it? How does it work?"

Bob stops for a moment, staring at the ceiling and apparently deep in thought. A few seconds pass, and then he looks down directly at you and responds, "Well, we'll have to model what you do. In essence, we have to capture all your bad behaviors."

Again you both start laughing. This time it's you that's choking. "Oh, no… I'm doomed!"

Bob continues, totally deadpan now, "No… You're safe as long as you keep paying me. But seriously, we have to model your various problem-solving methodologies and in doing so, map that methodology onto an intelligent processing engine."

You respond, "I wasn't aware such things were possible. Where did this come from?"

"Oh, the basic concepts have been around for some time. However, only recently have the required computational resources become commonly available." Bob then smiles a bit enigmatically and adds, "It's actually my specialty, one of my secret weapons in fact, and here's how it works…"

## The AI Thing

By this time, you're likely wondering, "What is this 'AI' thing, and how can it possibly help me meet my sales quota?" That's actually two questions, and in this chapter, we're going to deal with the first. We'll get to the second in due course, but before doing so, we're going to peek at the internals of AI and see what makes it tick.

I'll state at the outset that the subject can be highly technical as some of the most brilliant minds in modern human history have been involved. However, as with most good ideas, the core is elegant and simple, and for our purposes, that's all we'll need. It's so simple, in fact, that I can pretty much guarantee you'll come away with a clear understanding of how this thing works.

"AI," "artificial intelligence"—the name is actually something of a misnomer, mainly because no one understands exactly what "intelligence" is, let alone any "artificial" variation on the theme. However, it is suggestive. If we generally associate intelligence with problem-solving behavior, things make more sense because we all understand what it is to solve problems. Everyone does this every day. Furthermore, with this association, the adjective "artificial" makes sense as well because that simply suggests something other than the human mind as a problem-solving agent.

Do such things exist? Yes, they do. That's where the computers come in. Are these computers actually intelligent, like HAL-9000 from *2001* or the android Data from *Star Trek*? No, not quite yet, but they can intelligently solve at least some classes of problems. The distinction is important because (1) we really don't know what intelligence is and (2) these computers are using what amounts to a *model* of human problem-solving methodology. It's entirely possible to write computer programs that closely emulate how we solve problems. It isn't just about logic either, because as you already know, we humans can be clever. That's the punchline: AI is about computer programs that solve big problems cleverly.

Think about why we need to be clever in our various problem-solving behaviors. That's simple. It's because some problems are "hard" or "difficult." And why might these problems be regarded as difficult? Typically, it's about an inherent complexity. For example, they might involve tangled logic, many degrees of freedom (variables), statistical interdependencies, or incomplete information (i.e., we have to "guess"). Any or all of these attributes might trigger a need to be clever.

So what then does it mean to be clever? This is an interesting question, profound even because our hypothetical AI computer program will have to incorporate design principles that model "clever" behavior. As one might expect, defining "clever" is not so easy. In fact, this is itself a "difficult" problem, but we have an advantage in that we can observe ourselves "being clever" while engaged in solving various problems and learn from that.

More specifically, we can look for characteristic behavioral patterns in terms of expressed strategy and tactics, and from those patterns, extract a set of fundamental principles that allow us to think about modeling problem-solving methodology as a discipline in its own right. Much AI research concerns exactly this. Immediately, one might wonder if such modeling is even possible because humans can be exceedingly diverse in how they might approach a given problem. However, it turns out we humans employ a standard body of "tricks" that can be tailored to broad classes of problems and then represented as a set of actions on data representations encoded in the form of a computer program. The emphasis here is on "clever," and this motivates AI system design at all levels of abstraction.

The implication is that AI programs are somehow different than the standard procedural computer programs you might already be familiar with. Procedural code exhibits a fixed logic completely determined by input data. Examples include Excel, Word, or even your favorite web browser. In contrast, AI systems exhibit a more flexible, multitier logic whereby an execution pathway depends on the evolution of internal state. This is a sort of "logic-on-logic," if you will. Think of AI as a computer program that processes itself processing your data and then decides what to do next based on how that might be going. If this sounds complex, it really isn't. It's just that we can write programs that in some sense "look at themselves" (i.e., have a constant state of awareness) and thus determine how best to seek a solution state. We actually do the same thing when we step back and regard our own progress: If we're doing well, we'll keep doing whatever we're doing. If we're not doing so well, we might then make a change.

Amazingly, we've actually been able to create architecturally sophisticated AI programs for some time now, with computer languages (e.g., C, C$^{++}$, Java, Prolog, and Lisp), and software development tools (e.g., GCC, JDK, Visual Studio, and Eclipse), that have existed for decades. Our equation only lacked two things: (1) raw processing power and (2) data—lots of data. However, we're getting ahead of ourselves. First, let's take a more detailed look at the key components of an AI program because this will help us understand the real power of it.

So, let's drill down. Think about how you might go about solving a difficult problem. First, you might shoo away that bothersome, nagging coworker, lean back in your chair, and then attempt to visualize the problem. Right away, just by "visualizing," you're also creating an abstract representation, presumably to get down to the essentials of what you want to do and what you know, and thereby eliminating anything extraneous. Exactly how you might do this is up to you. You might look at things as a simple list of "IF-THEN-ELSE" statements (predicates), or as a word problem akin to those in a high school algebra class (natural language), or possibly as a network of interconnected things, each element of which expresses hierarchy and some set of attributes (geometry).

There are other possibilities as well. The point is, you will employ some form of representational schema as a convenient abstraction for the problem at hand. You might not think of it in such terms, but the advantages are immediately apparent because the representational form or format you choose makes things easier. Among other things, your representation is easily manipulated as you think things through. You can always tell "where you are" in terms of assumptions you've made, "where you're going" in terms of what to do next, and how close you are to something that resembles a solution. Furthermore, there is a fundamental equivalency in play implicit in your original problem visualization. Solve your representation, and you solve your problem. This is true "by construction," meaning that you've created the visualization with exactly this equivalency in mind. You're very clever in all this, and so is "the machine." After all, AI is modeling your problem-solving behavior. Thus, AI will also employ an abstract problem representation and for all the same reasons you do.

Now, returning to our armchair scenario, once you've visualized the problem, you then ask yourself "What do I know?" You consider the list of available facts pertinent to the problem at hand. Typically, the information accrues in a form such as "this thing or that thing is 'true' or 'false,'" "this or that thing has value such-and-such," or "this thing or that thing has attributes and is connected to some other thing that has attributes." You immediately apply this information to the problem representation you've adopted. Basically, you "hang tags" or "fill in the blanks" on as many components of your representation as might be possible and then ask yourself, "Have I solved my problem, and if not, what do I do now?" AI systems do this as well; they update free variables present in the problem representation (i.e., fill in "blanks"), and then assess "state" (i.e., determine configuration and solution status).

Thus, we see much of what an AI system does is dynamically manipulate "state" by temporarily assigning values in search of some combination that qualifies as a solution, again referencing the assumed problem representation. This constitutes what is generally known as a "search," and this term is illustrative in that it implies some form of goal-directed behavior. That is, we (1) consider "what to do next," (2) do that thing, and (3) assess the result and adjust the subsequent "what to do next" accordingly. For an AI system, this all translates to making new assumptions within the context of the search. As with most things, simply stated, "the Devil is in the details." The kicker is exactly how this "search" is done.

Okay. We're at a point where you've already explored "what you know." Obviously then, solution must somehow lay with "what you don't know." This implies the presence of free variables ("blanks") in the problem representation for which there are currently no assigned values. That is, you don't know whether such-and-such is "true" or "false" or "how big it is," or whatever. What to do? Well, if you're like me, you'll gather more evidence and then make a calculated guess at values for the most critical variables (blanks). This implies you'll proceed in a structured manner. You've already learned that being haphazard in attempting to solve difficult problems typically results in failure or frustration because you'll invariably forget "where you are" (i.e., all the assumptions you've made) and then have to do it all over again. Thus, you've "learned the hard way" to be conservative and careful. You'll organize all unknowns and systematically assign values so that all possibilities are covered. You'll do this one at a time and with each such change, recheck your solution state. You may even prioritize variables according to significance, or most likely values, or ancillary evidence of one form or another. That would be a clever set of tactics on your part and thus reveal you to be a commendably smart individual. This is the essence of "search." It's a "smart" thing that leverages all available information to find a path leading to a solution in the most efficient manner possible.

Unsurprisingly, AI systems model this same search behavior. However, AI goes one step further in leveraging some useful mathematics that you may not be aware of. AI represents all possible combinations of problem variables as a network consisting of "nodes" and "arcs," also called a "search-graph" or "search-space." This may be visualized as analogous to the interconnected structure of a fishnet, with "threads" corresponding to *connections* between things and "knots" where the threads join corresponding to those *things* that are in fact interconnected. The AI version is a bit more complex in that it is multidimensional to an arbitrarily high degree. This is a bit more difficult to visualize, but the principle is the same. The point to this analogy is twofold: (1) each "knot" (node) represents a given set of assumptions with blanks filled-in, and (2) each thread (arc) indicates some possible incremental change to that set of assumptions. In this manner, just by visiting a sequence of nodes via some pathway along the arcs, you always know "what to do next" based on the arcs present at any node. You also keep track of everything you've already done because you can always backtrack and remind yourself, or better yet save node visitations on a list and refer to it as needed. In effect, you in some sense wander through this network and thus visit all possibilities. "OK!", you might say. "But why do we need it?" Primarily because the abstraction we've created enables *maximally efficient search*. This is critical because the sort of problems we assign to an AI may require processing massive amounts of data. Therefore, efficiency is a must.

For an AI system, the aforementioned generation and exploration of pathways in this mathematical search-space constitutes a formal definition of what is known as "search." As we've defined search, it might even be considered a prime function of AI because this is the fundamental mechanism by which all free variables that might render solution to the original problem are accessed and assigned values. Of course, search-space can still be exceedingly complex, and we want to find the solution state as quickly as possible. That's where the "clever" comes in because AI will also seek evidence from the data to choose one path versus another. We begin to glimpse the power of AI in that it provides a means for the systematic exploration of this search-space for problems of arbitrary size. This implies that very complex problems well beyond ordinary human capabilities might be addressed in this manner. As I've already stated, the possibilities are endless. However, it gets even better.

**Domain Expertise of Sales**

However, the discussion so far has been misleading in a key respect: real-world problems are rarely so straightforward. In particular, while we may reasonably expect an AI system to denote at least some logical conditions under which a solution state might exist, there remains the problem of incomplete data. In other words, our original input is insufficient for straightforward problem solution. This can easily happen even in the simplest systems where input data generates ambiguity in the form of multiple possible solutions, or even engenders support for solutions that contradict one another. Under such circumstances, "search" alone is incapable of generating what we might regard as a usable solution, mainly because despite its power, it will still generate those same ambiguous or even contradictory solutions and then go no further. Before we tackle this serious issue, let's take another look at our initial set of assumptions about our problem.

What is the nature of the aforementioned assumptions, exactly? What types of information do they contain? Well, as we return to sitting in our chair, visualizing the problem, we discern two distinct components: (1) "statements of fact" (i.e., to which values may be assigned), and (2) how those facts might relate to one another in generating a solution. The former identifies variables that are present in the problem formulation and delimits values those variables might assume. Some values may actually be provided on input (e.g., via direct user interface or more commonly, a database query). Others will be generated by the AI itself (e.g., within the context of a search). This component also forms the basis of our problem representation.

The latter tells us what to do with those facts once values have been assigned, and it's critical to note that such information is not actually an input to our hypothetical AI system. Rather, it is pre-encoded as a *domain expertise* that allows the system to consider evidence in support of one assumption versus another, or one conclusion versus another. This forms the basis of a "knowledge representation." This knowledge representation construct encodes domain expertise in the form of actions to be taken based on the AI system's internal state (configuration). As used here, "internal state" includes the current set of variable assignments (problem representation), where the system might be in the solution process (search), and what the solution process looks like thus far (configuration). Stated differently, the knowledge representation encodes strategic and tactical expertise specific to the problem domain (e.g., "sales"). As such, it becomes a final arbiter of "what to do next" within the context of solution-search. This is actually the root of the "clever" we need. Interestingly, knowledge representation domain specificity forms the means by which an AI system is tailored to the solution of problems belonging to a certain category or class. Your "sales" AI system isn't just "brute force"; it will incorporate lots of "lessons learned" from the sales domain. It will have learned from you.

But, what then is domain expertise, really? Part of it is just facts. For example, a successful salesperson will have lots of facts at hand pertaining to what Customer XYZ has done in the past—what she's purchased, when she purchased, and who might have done the purchasing. However, this isn't all of it. That same salesperson will also have some sense of what that customer (or, perhaps another customer in some sense similar) might do given some set of historical facts. Thus, that salesperson is capable of thinking in terms of "confidence" or "probability," and this is the missing ingredient to resolving ambiguity or even contradiction.

The fact is, when we think about solving a given problem, we often have at hand several possible conclusions, but any action is predicated on what we think is the most likely solution. That is, we "weigh the odds." Thinking in such terms is fundamentally tolerant of ambiguity and contradiction. AI systems do the same, but they use mathematics to formalize and systematize the reasoning process. In this case, where our knowledge representation is in the form of the aforementioned IF-THEN-ELSE statements, an explicit probabilistic reasoning in the form of

Bayesian networks or fuzzy logic may be used. Where the problem can be reduced to one of pattern classification, an implicit method such as an Artificial Neural Network (ANN) to which a classification probability is attached might be employed. The upshot is, just as we're able to do, *the AI system effectively reasons under ambiguity.*[5] The practical result is we can expect actionable results from the AI system in the form of possible solutions to our problem, each of which is ranked according to a confidence calculated based on all available evidence.

"Hmm... All this sounds very good," you might say. "It sounds as if the machine can reason very effectively, but where does this 'evidence' come from? Do we have to add this to the knowledge representation up front? Is this something we have to enter as an input? If so, that doesn't sound like much of an improvement against me just sitting in my chair and ruminating on the 'state of the world.' After all, people in my position are very busy. We have customers to attend and deals to close. We don't have the time or inclination to just sit around spoon-feeding a machine stuff we already know, and better than anyone else, I might add." Point taken. You've put your finger on one reason AI technology didn't take off years ago, but things are different now. Aside from lots more processing power, we also have access to data, massive amounts of it. The implication is you don't have to "spoon-feed" data to the machine. Rather, just tell it "where to look" and "how to look." Now, if that sounds difficult, I can make it very simple; just plug that CAT-5 cable into the LAN connector on your computer.

Well, it's not quite *that* simple, but close. You'll still need a bit of software. In particular, the AI system designer will have to

---

[5] See Glossary at the end of the book for definitions on selected terms that will be used throughout this book.

add structure to the knowledge representation that informs the AI system of a means to obtain evidence. This is where "Big Data" comes in. We'll get into the details of Big Data later, but suffice to say at this point, adding a knowledge representation component pertaining to the means by which evidence is obtained is highly compact and also scalable, far more so than the data itself. The modern AI system has access to virtually unlimited amounts of data that might pertain to confidence in or the probability of a particular result. This is but one of the major advances of the Big Data revolution and one of the essential factors giving the new AI its practical applications.

How is this actually done? The details are irrelevant here. However, much of what might qualify as evidence accrues as patterns of one form or another. Thus, evidence is rendered logically equivalent to *patterns in the raw data* that may or may not be present. You've probably heard of all the recent hype surrounding Machine Learning, Artificial Neural Networks (ANN), or even Convolutional Neural Networks (CNN). Well, this is the reason why. Computer scientists have figured out a way to apply these technologies at scale, enabling efficient acquisition of evidence in the form of advanced analytics. A key point is these analytics are also informed by the staggering amount of data available on Internet, and your AI system will directly access this resource. Yet another important point is that those same ANN and CNN constructs qualify as a type of knowledge representation, of which the modern AI will typically incorporate several.

So, what do we have thus far? Just how good is our AI system at performing the various tasks we envision? Well, we're not quite done with our breakdown, but I can already answer: "The AI system will perform as well as the knowledge representation permits." Now, this response may seem flippant, enigmatic, logically circular, or even disingenuous. However, there is a method to the madness. There is no magic here, but there is ample sophistication. In particular, recall that the AI system is intended to model intelligent problem-solving behaviors. Thus, we are the teachers, and if we are sufficiently clever in the creation of such a model, our AI system may perform very well indeed and at scale extending far beyond normal human capability.

In practical terms, once a problem-solving methodology is abstracted in logical form, it all comes down to implementation based on established principles of systems design: mathematics, logic, and computer algorithms. Furthermore, AI systems may be trained so that *performance incrementally improves with each iteration*. This capability forms yet another critical component of the knowledge representation. That is to say, the AI system may be constructed as self-correcting in the modification of its own structure. In effect, AI incorporates a capability to add new logical relations. In the software world, this is what separates AI from all the rest. In principle, this training may be extended toward a limiting perfection within a given domain of applicability. This is real, and it's here now.

Yet we're still not quite finished with this knowledge representation. Think about those really hard problems you've attempted to solve, the ones that seemed so difficult they might as well be regarded as impossible. Like a Rubik's Cube, you turn it this way and that, and nothing seems to work. You keep at it, though, and at some point, you suddenly realize what you're looking at is more than one problem. That is, you see it as composed of pieces, subproblems if you will, that when jointly solved also solve the larger, original problem.

Now, if you follow this tack, you're then faced with multiple problems, possibly still quite difficult. However, each of those subproblems is already more simple than the original, and indeed, if those subproblems prove too difficult, you can apply the same process again. This technique is called *recursive problem decomposition*. It's all the rage, and all the smartest people are doing it. First, you decompose the problem into subproblems, and then if those subproblems remain difficult, you just do it again. At some point, the subproblems you've generated are simple, and with all tools at hand, you then solve those problems forthwith. This entire process is called "Scatter."

You've also kept track of any problem decompositions thus implemented. Consequently, you also know how to reassemble solutions to any decomposition you've generated, in succession, all the way up to the original problem. This is called "Gather," effectively the inverse process of "Scatter." This combination is hereafter referred to as *scatter-gather*. This is an exceedingly powerful technique, and AI systems already possess this capability as a basic architectural feature.

How is this done? Simple: We add yet another component to our knowledge representation pertaining to conditions under which scatter-gather may be usefully applied. Accordingly, the AI system will scan its own internal state, and where such conditions are detected, the scatter-gather process is initiated. Thus, we arrive at the pièce de résistance of our encoded knowledge-representation. Remember, this is a behavior that you routinely employ in successful problem solving, and what's more, this behavior is also encodable as a programming construct we then append to our AI system. You likely didn't think of it this way when you were doing it, but like you, the AI system will sometimes simplify the solution process by employing what amounts to a "break the problem into pieces" tactic. That is, the AI will effectively "call itself" and in doing so, impose a new (sub)problem representation at each stage of recursion. And, when all subproblems are thus solved, the AI will backtrack to reassemble a complete solution to the original problem.

Waxing visionary for just a moment, there is no reason why other AI systems encoding different domains of expertise cannot be invoked in this manner. Following the idea to a logical conclusion, we then have AI systems worldwide jointly performing intelligent processing on problems of massive scale. You may have noticed something else. There's no need to sequentially process those subproblems generated during scatter-gather. Rather, they can at any stage be processed "in-parallel," enabling a substantial speed-up. This parallel processing capability is a fundamental attribute of all supercomputing systems. Thus, our hypothetical, worldwide AI network is also a supercomputer. Now from a "hard-nosed-strictly-practical" point of view, is it unrealistic to expect such a system might help meet sales quotas? Well, perhaps such a conjecture is too far a stretch, unless of course one is selling worldwide to a customer base numbering in the tens of thousands, and from a highly diverse product portfolio. Just so you know, this could be done today. And again, the possibilities are endless.

So, let's take stock of what we have. The AI system we've been describing is nothing more than a computer program designed to emulate human problem-solving behavior within a particular domain of expertise. For example, this AI system could manifest as an intelligent advisor for generating, pursuing, and developing sales leads. In what follows, we'll explore this particular idea much further but for now, just remember that this AI system does something useful in a given domain. And, what might that "something useful" be? Generally speaking, in using the AI system, we offload at least some portion of those "WTDN" or "What-To-Do-Next" type problems that accrue in our work. This WTDN category is typified by a need for upfront, "smart" problem-solving as a precursor to the solution of more straightforward problems that can be solved using standard algorithmic techniques.

For example, it's simple to extrapolate a customer's need for a given product during the next quarter, based on trends developed over previous quarters. Generating such an extrapolation requires no intelligence at all; merely press a button on the canned linear regression algorithm in your Excel spreadsheet. However, anticipating a customer's needs before a business relationship has even been established is something altogether different. In such cases, any information that might be available is public domain and typically of a more tenuous nature. Examples might include diverse and seemingly disparate clues such as market trends, patent filings, published papers and presentations, dynamic connections with other companies, social media traffic, corporate advisory board membership, and purchasing patterns of a more generic nature on the part of companies that may be regarded as somehow similar. The point is that *any anticipation under such circumstances requires application of a high-order intelligence.*

Now, here's the central thrust to everything we're saying: Humans possess an inherent capability to reason effectively based on sparse or uncertain data, and AI systems can be developed to model this same capability. This is their fundamental utility. Furthermore, AI systems by construction are systematic in application of problem-solving methodology and are also capable of processing at virtually unlimited scale. Simply stated, they're completely dogged, never becoming tired or distracted. They can't replace you, but to the extent that your workflow demands intelligent problem-solving behavior, they can help you with an effective multiplication of the intelligence you already have.

Now, we've introduced many terms and concepts, and you may feel a bit overwhelmed. So, before we go on, let's summarize what we know so far:

- AI systems are nothing more than a type of computer program.

- AI computer programs are architected differently to accommodate what we might call a *non-procedural logic*. Stated differently, they don't always "flow" in the same way; just like us, they flexibly adapt problem-solving behavior depending on type and quality of any data at hand.

- An AI system functions by generating a series of candidate solutions and then testing to see if solution criteria are met.

- AI systems are composed of standard architectural components. What this means is that there's nothing magic here, just a standard set of computer-programmable, machine-readable "chunks" cleverly composed but still subject to our analysis and understanding. We can list those components here: (1) problem representation, (2) knowledge representation, (3) solution search, (4) problem/sub-problem decomposition, (5) scatter-gather recursion, and (6) a set of methods by which internal state and solution state may be calculated or assessed.

**Meta-Sales**

In the previous discussion, the problem domain-space was more or less implicit to problem and knowledge representations. However, domain space is worthy of a particular emphasis because it establishes the terms of solution search via expression of all variables pertinent to problem solution. Some set of domain variables will be specified on input; however, this set may be augmented by the AI system itself, as processing unfolds.

These domain variables may refer to entities being subjected to various analyses, dependent attributes, relations, or analytics. At first blush, this definition might seem vague, but that's only because a domain has not been specified. That is, to the extent a problem is posed within a specific domain, one of the ways an AI system is rendered specific to that domain is by virtue of the assumed set of domain variables. For example, in the sales world, we would be talking about some company or commercial interest as a potential client, for which relevant attributes might include all the data elements one would find on a corporate balance sheet, plus products, market penetration, technology utilization, executive management, current projects, funding sources, etc. Pertinent relations might include "is a customer of," "is a subsidiary of," "is funded by," or where web-pages are considered, "is hyperlinked to/from." Thus defined, the set of all domain variables in turn defines a node-construct that the AI system can manipulate and by which the solution search-space representation may then be generated.

The knowledge representation encodes logic pertinent to the application of search in identifying an acceptable solution to our question or query. That query might be any of an effectively infinite variety. For example, we might ask something as pointed as "What specific electronic components are Company XYZ likely to purchase in the next quarter?" Alternatively, we might ask something as general as "What new markets will Company XYZ be serving next year?" or even "What new technology will Company XYZ purchase over the next 10 years?"

Is the AI system is capable of handling such wide variation? Yes. Where natural language processing is employed, a more or less free-form query can in principle be supported. Even with a formatted input, the AI system will still be able to process the query, assuming supporting knowledge representation components are available. Once a query is accepted as actionable, the AI system then applies the knowledge representation in search of a solution to that query. In doing so, the AI system models how we might think about such things. Among other considerations, this implies the knowledge representation incorporates *knowledge about how to acquire knowledge*. Stated differently, the AI system knows how to look for relationships that might substantiate a solution. In the parlance of philosophers, logicians, and AI practitioners, this touches on a form of *metaknowledge* or even *metalogic*, a logic about logic.

My guess is that a clear picture is beginning to emerge concerning all this AI stuff. To wit, "The AI system leverages a knowledge representation in order to explore my problem domain in a purposeful manner. Thus, exploration becomes a solution-search by which all relevant information is exposed in identifying an answer to my question." In effect, the knowledge representation serves to define a line of inquiry in the form of what might be cast as a *search trajectory* by which the AI system may proceed from one set of assumptions to another in amassing evidence for one conclusion versus another.

For example, suppose we're attempting to answer the question "What new components will Company XYZ purchase next quarter?" To answer that question, we might then ask a series of questions: "What new products are Company XYZ building?",

"From whom have they purchased components in the past?", "To whom are they selling?", "What technologies are involved?", and "What components are needed for products expressing technology ABC?" Answers to all these questions might be found via a sufficiently sophisticated solution-search within a sufficiently rich domain representation. "Ah ha!", so you say. "That's merely theoretical. 'Solution-in-Principle' doesn't help me. 'Sufficiently Sophisticated' and 'Sufficiently Rich' don't help me. Don't even attempt to fool me. Can we *really* do this?" Yes, we can do it. That's yet another juncture where Big Data will come in.

So, what about the remaining pieces: "problem/sub-problem decomposition," "scatter-gather," and "calculation of solution-state"? Recall the previous example of the Rubik's Cube, where one must break the problem into subproblems. Back in the 'hood, we called this "breaking it down." In this earthy metaphor, one more knowledge representation component is implied, one that accommodates alternate representations based on problem decomposition. This would constitute a distinct knowledge category that informs of junctures within solution search where posing of an equivalent set of subproblems may prove fortuitous.

The possible benefit here is both tactical and practical—"tactical" because the overall problem solution may be simplified via an opportunistic reduction in number of degrees of freedom (i.e., the number of variables one must simultaneously manage), and "practical" because the subproblems are independent by definition and thus may be solved more quickly, all at the same time. Does this work for every problem? No, but many problems can be treated this way, and where applicable, the benefits can be massive. Now, if subproblem decomposition is indeed applicable, "scatter-gather" is the mechanism through which the solution of subproblems is managed. In effect, once the subproblem representation is assembled, our AI system recursively calls itself for each subproblem, and then once all subproblems are solved falls back (returns) to the original invocation and stitches together (assembles) a complete solution. This is powerful, brilliant stuff and provides much of the power of AI. Note also that the subproblems are independent of each other, which implies that scatter-gather is consistent with supercomputer-styled parallel-processing. The implications are huge. In particular, this is one of the most significant bridges to the IoT/Big Data world.

Now, as a final piece, we need to know when we've arrived at a solution. As one might expect, "solution" is a special type of state, and as such, it also has a representation. This "solution representation" incorporates termination criteria and is logically associated with the problem representation. This makes sense because a problem representation is reasonably expected to include a means to ascertain when a problem is indeed solved. The AI system will actually leverage the solution representation in two ways: (1) to know when it's done and (2) to know when it's close to being done. The former will terminate processing (unless, that is, multiple solutions are indicated), and the latter will help guide further solution search. Thus, there is a dynamic aspect to the solution representation in that it is updated, scanned, and evaluated at every incremental search step. This is the mechanism by which the AI system informs itself of having reached a solution state. Once an acceptable solution is found, the complete solution representation is then scanned in the generation of useful output.

Having explored how AI technology really works, we're now well equipped to further consider how it can help with a given job. "Sales Ex Machina" – "Sales from a Machine"… Is this really possible? In fact, it is already a reality. Does this technology promise to replace sales personnel? The answer is "no," but it can help sales personnel to become better. Some will even become "sales superstars" as a result of the clever application of this technology, and it could be you.

# CHAPTER 1

# Data Exhaust – Big Data Is Small Data

*Every client, voluntarily or involuntarily, is constantly emitting discrete information into the datasphere. Alone, this data reveals little; in aggregate, it reveals their intention, motivation, and true state.*

Let's turn our attention to what fuels any Machine Learning system. Data! How much data do you produce on a daily basis? Most people have never taken the time to think about the vast amount of information that a system is gathering on you. The amount of data you produce (data exhaust) is incalculable.

To give you a simple example, let's take a look at the amount of information you could be uploading to the system from the moment you wake up to the moment you arrive at your job.

| Data Source | Data Collected: |
|---|---|
| Alarm | Time you go to bed |
| | Time you wake up |
| | Snooze button (x times) |
| | Sound source (tone, music, news, weather) |
| Lights | When did you turn them off |
| | When did you turn them on |
| | Which lights did you turn on |
| | Which lights did you turn on first/last |
| | How many rooms |
| | Number of lights per room |
| Shower | Time of day |
| | Temperature |
| | Length |
| | # of gallons consumed |
| Coffee | When did you turn it on |
| | Scoops of coffee |
| | Type of coffee |
| | Cups consumed |
| | Time between cups |
| Refrigerator | Time of day |
| | # of times you opened it |
| | Time intervals (time between openings) |
| | What you consumed |
| | How much you consumed |
| Stove | Time of day |
| | Number of burners |
| | Settings |
| | Cooking time |
| | Temperatures |
| | Energy (electrical or gas) consumed |
| Internet | Time of day |

|  | Browser |
|---|---|
|  | Home location |
|  | Websites visited |
|  | Duration on each site |
|  | Videos, articles, and audio consumed |
|  | Links clicked |
|  | Keyword searches |
|  | Close browsers |
| Thermostat | Settings |
|  | # of times you change it |
|  | When you leave the house (timestamp) |
|  | When you return home (timestamp) |
|  | Home energy consumption |
| Door | Number of open/closes |
|  | Number of times left open and for how long |
|  | Time it's locked or unlocked |
| Car | Day of the week |
|  | Distance |
|  | Time in traffic |
|  | # of hard brakes |
|  | Average speed |
|  | # of accelerations |
|  | # of stops |
|  | Length of time of stops |
|  | Temperature in the car |
|  | Radio stations (types: news, weather, etc.) |
|  | Smoke detection (tobacco, vaping, marijuana) |
|  | # of right turns vs. left turns |
|  | Time between signal-stop-turn |
| ATM | Time of day |
|  | How much is withdrawn |

| | Number of withdrawals per week |
|---|---|
| | Location(s) |
| | Photo image |
| Starbucks | What did you order? |
| | Receipt amount(s) |
| | # of times a week |
| | Location(s) |
| Mobile | How many calls |
| | Length of calls |
| | Battery life |
| | Signal strength |
| | Videos viewed; kinds of videos and source(s) |
| | Music heard; kinds of music and source(s) |
| Job | Time of arrival |
| | Time between arrival and exiting the car |

This is only a sample of how much data can potentially be collected in a 2–3 hour period. Imagine how much data is collected in one day, week, month, or year. Other data sources could potentially include traffic cameras, gas stations, grocery stores, restaurants, fast food chains, retail stores, malls, strip malls, repair shops, salons, and barbers; the list can go on and on.

The sum total of all this scattered data, if such a thing were ever assembled (i.e., gathered), is how much data you're potentially emitting into the digital ecosystem. How much of this data is yours? 100%. How much of it do you own? 0%. How will this data be used? Well, that depends on who has the data and what their intentions might be.

**Target Knows Before It Shows**

Every time you go shopping and swipe that credit card, retail stores are taking note of what you're buying. Every item you buy is tracked and pegged to your "buying persona." Like an electronic Sherlock Holmes, the system is piecing together clues about who you are, your tendencies, your preferences, and, in sum, your buying habits. The system is algorithmically motivated to find patterns in your buying behavior so that it can predict what you'll be inclined to purchase next. This is an obvious and reasonable gambit.

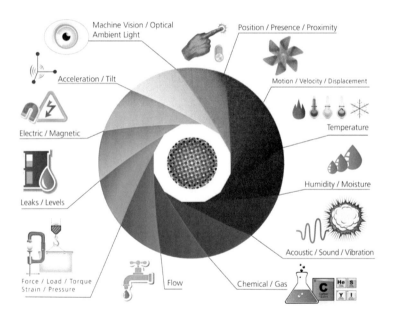

**Figure 2: IoT Data Sensors and Actuators by Postscapes.com**

Here's a simple data model you may be able to relate to. You go into your local Starbucks and order a latte. You also decide to buy a nice classic donut to go with it. Now, aside from having your name, credit card number, email, and/or mobile number,

Starbucks is at least capturing the following data: time of purchase, item(s) purchased (SKU #), and method of payment (Target Credit Card, American Airlines Credit Card, Delta American Express, and so on). From a weather data source, it can also collect what type of day it was when you made that purchase. Was it a sunny day or cloudy? Precipitation? Average temperature for your area?

The system is constantly updating your buying persona with every purchase. Think of every item you buy as a data point that a machine uses as a variable to calculate your buying behavior. I could go on with this, but the point is that any data deemed salient to the conditions under which you might purchase something is grist for the mill (i.e., possibly recorded and associated with you).

The more data points (i.e., the more data exhaust you emit) the system has, the more it can begin to "learn," via machine language, who you are. The system gets smarter about you with every purchase you make.

All these data points, whether directly emitted by you through your purchases or indirectly (e.g., weather) begins to give the system some idea of your buying patterns (what you buy) and your buying habits (when you buy). Using Predictive Models in the form of a computer algorithm, the system can then begin to draw some conclusions as to what you will need in the future. The system is with surprising effectiveness able to anticipate what you want to buy before you've decided what to buy.

Here's an example of what we're talking about. Several years ago the retail giant Target gave us a glimpse into the future use of small data and how Machine Learning will be able to anticipate your needs before you can.

For every client, Target assigns an ID that's tied to their credit card. The credit card information is linked to your address (geography), email, mobile number, age, gender, marital status, income, credit card score, and other things we haven't even thought of yet. Add to this list of data points the number of data sources (e.g., public lists or data sets) Target has purchased, which further adds to the predictive power of their system.

In a *New York Times* article, Charles Duhigg, author of *The Power of Habits*, shares a story on how deep the data rabbit hole goes when it comes to collecting data on you.[6] This example is a harbinger of the changes that are coming in the world of retail and more specifically, selling.

> Andrew Pole had just started working as a statistician for Target in 2002, when two colleagues from the marketing department stopped by his desk to ask an odd question: *"If we wanted to figure out if a customer is pregnant, even if she didn't want us to know, can you do that?"* (emphasis added)
>
> Pole has a master's degree in statistics and another in economics, and has been obsessed with the intersection of data and human behavior most of his life.
>
> As the marketers explained to Pole… new parents are a retailer's holy grail. Most shoppers don't buy everything they need at one store. Instead, they buy groceries at the grocery store and toys at the toy store, and they visit Target only when they need certain items they associate with Target — cleaning supplies, new socks or a six-month supply of toilet paper. But Target sells everything from milk to stuffed animals to lawn furniture to electronics, so one of the company's primary goals is

---

[6] Duhigg, Charles. "How Companies Learn Your Secrets." *The New York Times.* Feb. 16, 2012. http://www.nytimes.com/2012/02/19/magazine/shopping-habits.html?pagewanted=1&_r=1&hp

convincing customers that the only store they need is Target. But it's a tough message to get across, even with the most ingenious ad campaigns, because once consumers' shopping habits are ingrained, it's incredibly difficult to change them.

There are, however, some brief periods in a person's life when old routines fall apart and buying habits are suddenly in flux. One of those moments — the moment, really — is right around the birth of a child, when parents are exhausted and overwhelmed and their shopping patterns and brand loyalties are up for grabs. But as Target's marketers explained to Pole, timing is everything. Because birth records are usually public, the moment a couple have a new baby, they are almost instantaneously barraged with offers and incentives and advertisements from all sorts of companies. which means that the key is to reach them earlier, before any other retailers know a baby is on the way. Specifically, *the marketers said they wanted to send specially designed ads to women in their second trimester*, which is when most expectant mothers begin buying all sorts of new things, like prenatal vitamins and maternity clothing. "Can you give us a list?" the marketers asked.

"*We knew that if we could identify them in their second trimester, there's a good chance we could capture them for years*," Pole told me. "As soon as we get them buying diapers from us, they're going to start buying everything else too. If you're rushing through the store, looking for bottles, and you pass orange juice, you'll grab a carton. Oh, and there's that new DVD I want. Soon, you'll be buying cereal and paper towels from us, and keep coming back."

The desire to collect information on customers is not new for Target or any other large retailer, of course. For decades, Target has collected vast amounts of data on every person who regularly walks into one of its stores. Whenever possible, Target assigns each shopper a unique code—known internally as the Guest ID number—that keeps tabs on everything they buy. "If you use a credit card or a coupon, or fill out a survey, or mail in a refund, or call the customer help line, or open an e-mail we've sent to you or visit our Web site, we'll record it and link it to your Guest ID," Pole said. "We want to know everything we can."

How much data is being collected on you? The article continues:

Also linked to your Guest ID is demographic information like your age, whether you are married and have kids, which part of town you live in, how long it takes you to drive to the store, your estimated salary, whether you've moved recently, what credit cards you carry in your wallet and what Web sites you visit. Target can buy data about your ethnicity, job history, the magazines you read, if you've ever declared bankruptcy or got divorced, the year you bought (or lost) your house, where you went to college, what kinds of topics you talk about online, whether you prefer certain brands of coffee, paper towels, cereal or applesauce, your political leanings, reading habits, charitable giving and the number of cars you own. (In a statement, Target declined to identify what demographic information it collects or purchases.) *All that information is meaningless without someone to analyze and make sense of it.* That's where Andrew Pole and the dozens of other members of Target's Guest Marketing Analytics department come in.

And how is Target using this data? How invasive can this data collection get? Duhigg continues the story of a man who went to the Target store in Minneapolis requesting to speak with the manager. The man wasn't happy and here's why:

> "My daughter got this in the mail!" he said. "She's still in high school, and you're sending her coupons for baby clothes and cribs? Are you trying to encourage her to get pregnant?"
>
> The manager didn't have any idea what the man was talking about. He looked at the mailer. Sure enough, it was addressed to the man's daughter and contained advertisements for maternity clothing, nursery furniture and pictures of smiling infants. The manager apologized and then called a few days later to apologize again.
>
> On the phone, though, the father was somewhat abashed. "I had a talk with my daughter," he said. "It turns out there's been some activities in my house I haven't been completely aware of. She's due in August. I owe you an apology."

Here's one more example of how the system is being used to anticipate your needs. Dennis Berman of the *Wall Street Journal* had the opportunity to interview Aetna's Chairman and CEO Mark Bertolini in a forum titled *The Future of Healthcare: On the Predictive Power of Today's Machine*.

The process of digitizing medical records is underway, and now retailers and insurance companies are using that information to determine what to sell to you and when. Bertolini said, "We know with a major retailer that people diagnosed with a Type 2 diabetes, generally within two–three weeks before being diagnosed, change laundry detergent beforehand because it causes their skin to itch and smell differently because their blood sugar is so high."[7]

We've all had that creepy feeling when we think of something and days later we get an email or direct mailer with a coupon invitation to stop by and indulge at a discounted rate. I like to call this moment "déjà knew" (already knew).[8] The system knew based on my online search queries, websites I'd visited, or recent purchases I'd made that I was in the mood for Italian food. The predictive power of the algorithm spit out my name, linked it to a partner provider (i.e., the nearby Italian restaurant), generated an email with a discount offer, and sent it to me. Number of humans involved? None. Number of data points involved in reaching that conclusion with such accuracy? Only the algorithm knows!

I mean that quite literally. With an unsupervised algorithm, the data points aren't labeled or predetermined; only the system really knows how many are needed to make that decision.

Now imagine for a moment that a salesperson had this type of predictive power at their fingertips. How would that change the salesperson's ability to sell more effectively? How would that change the salesperson's prospecting efforts? And further imagine how this *déjà knew* superpower would impact

---

[7] "The Future of: Healthcare," *Wall Street Journal*, Feb. 16, 2017
https://www.youtube.com/watch?v=vhap6VdBDKA

[8] Wikipedia: "Déjà vu from French, literally 'already seen', is the phenomenon of having the feeling that the situation currently being experienced has already been experienced in the past."

conversations with a client and the salesperson's ability to influence that client's decision-making process.

## Off-loading

Your company's internal database obviously has records of each and every one of your corporate clients. Those transactions are pulled into your CRM (Customer Relationship Management) system where you keep track of every interaction with your clients.

For example, a client hasn't bought anything in the last year. You've reached out several times, but you get voicemail every time and they never return your phone call. You've sent out several emails, but that hasn't been successful either. You have to make a decision: continue pursuing or not. You decide to stop reaching out because your sales pipeline is loaded with other qualified leads and you don't have the bandwidth to chase clients who are most likely not in the right stage of the buying cycle. As is common in the sales universe, you get busy with other active clients, and this particular client is then relegated by default to the "dead zone" (i.e., the forgotten account).

Now, what if we were to implement a machine learning algorithm to off-load these forgotten accounts as well as your current accounts? The goal of the system would be to find a way to reactivate (or reanimate) these dead accounts. How would this work? Imagine that your system was tied to external databases that track your client's activities outside your company's direct purview. For example, every industry has its share of magazines, blogs, online communities, newsletters, and websites that track trends, policy changes, press releases, new product or service introductions, and a host of other newsworthy items dedicated to what's going on in that particular industry.

Let's assume that your inactive customer is either a member of one of those organizations, a subscriber to a newsletter, an active commenter on those blogs, or all the above. What then if your client visited one of the social networking sites and engaged in a conversation about a particular topic that directly relates to what you're selling, and thereby creating salient data exhaust?

The system would sense sentiment and intent by capturing keywords or phrases that would allow it, through prescriptive processes, to automatically generate an email with a specific offering along with a subject line that's tied to the topic that was being discussed. How likely is it that this inactive customer would respond to your email? I would say highly likely, or at the very least, the client is reminded that you're still around and want their business.

The beauty (or, some would say "scary" thing) of machine learning is that the system itself is getting smarter with every piece of data it captures and consumes. In principle, no intervention is needed on the part of the salesperson. The system never stops monitoring or listening for new information to indicate that the client may be ready to make a purchase. It simply never gets tired of following up; it stays vigilant and never gets frustrated.

From the standpoint of a sales mindset, think about how this tool can compensate for human shortcomings:

- The system never gets frustrated; it never has a bad day.

- The system never gets tired of following up; it never has a low-energy day.

- The system never takes the lack of response personally; it never has a self-esteem issue.

- The system doesn't have to attend meetings; it never responds with the standard "day got away from me" excuse.

The ability of the system to take unstructured data exhaust from a variety of sources, format it into machine data, apply predictive analytics, and prescribe the Next-Best-Action (NBA) will allow salespeople to manage their time more effectively by allowing them to free up their mental (thinking about who to call next) and physical (calling or sending an email) efforts from working on low-probability clients and focus solely on clients who are more likely to buy than not.

Takeaways:

- You are generating data with every action or activity in your daily life.

- Data sources can include things external to you (e.g., weather, traffic patterns, etc.) and be used as part of some predictive algorithm.

- Scattered data is constantly being gathered to anticipate a buyer's or person's need as we saw in the Target example

- Off-loading follow-up tasks to a Machine Learning system can free up time for the salesperson to focus on qualified leads.

# CHAPTER 2

# Cognitive Calling – How AI Is Impacting Telemarketing

*Human intervention in the admittedly mundane task of moving a client along in the sales funnel is reaching a point where it can be handed over to a cognitive assistant, thereby freeing the salesperson to engage in the higher-level strategic and tactical sales-centric activities that only a human can do.*

Telemarketing is a function within a business that is dedicated to making outbound phone calls to existing or potential clients for the usual purpose of informing, selling, or prospecting. For example, if there is an election pending, political telemarketers will get on the phone and call likely voters to give them information on their party's candidate. The goal is to (a) give the resident more information to reassure them they're voting for the right candidate or (2) give them information to sway them to vote for the telemarketer's candidate. Simply put, the goal is to inform and in doing so, influence.

In other instances, telemarketers are using the phones to sell people on a variety of products or services:

- Cable TV Providers
- Internet Service Providers
- Home Security Systems
- Charitable Organizations
- Fund Raising

When telemarketers contact a resident about the above products or service, their goal is to facilitate a transaction via phone.

Another function of a telemarketing organization is prospecting for new clients or upselling existing clients. Typically, the immediate goal is persuading them to have a one-on-one meeting with one of the organization's sales representatives to "close the deal."

Industries that rely on prospecting via phone include, but are not limited to:

- Personal Financial Services
- Property Timeshares
- Financial Advisors
- Investment Opportunities

Distinctions notwithstanding, the overarching goal of telemarketing is selling. A political telemarketer is calling to sell the resident on sticking with their candidate or changing to the other candidate. A telemarketer who is seeking a one-on-one meeting is selling you on the value of taking time out of your day to sit with them.

The telemarketers who call are using a script to guide what they say and when to say it. "Script" here has its traditional meaning, a written dialogue or set of instructions for each stage of the call.

In the beginning, telemarketers worked from scripts on paper sheets or index cards. As the telemarketers engaged, they would quickly sift to the correct page or card to figure out what to say next. As you can imagine, this approach wasn't the most efficient or most fluid way of piecing together a natural flowing conversation. Often, telemarketers would read the wrong card or misplace it altogether and not know what to say. You can imagine how these awkward moments of silence eroded the subject's confidence, calling into question the legitimacy of the call itself.

This human error would often result in the subject simply hanging up and disconnecting the call—an embarrassing and counterproductive outcome. Obviously, this old system was inefficient to say the least.

Then there is the problem of *brittleness*, whereby a customer interaction based on canned responses is at best stilted and unnatural. In effect, there was no real way of tracking if the telemarketer was even saying the right things at the right time based on the subject's question or response.

Telemarketing companies eventually began to record the phone conversations and review them to maintain quality control. Some quality control was necessary, but this solution wasn't scalable. Imagine that one telemarketer makes 100 calls per day and manages to get 10 people on a call, with each conversation lasting thirty minutes; this results in about 5 hours of conversation every day. Multiply this daily number by the number of telemarketers you have, and you can see that it really isn't feasible (scalable). Admitting the futility of 100% quality control, the companies began to review only a sample of the conversations from those telemarketers who were struggling to sell or set up appointments. This approach still has many holes, but it was better than nothing.

The next step in the evolution of telemarketing was the use of computers. The paper and index cards were replaced by smart programs that allowed the telemarketer to click and open "mini-scripts," so he or she could adapt and respond quickly. The resulting conversations with the subject sounded far more casual and natural than the scripted and rehearsed version. For example, let's take a conversation a financial services telemarketer might have with a potential client. Upon hearing the potential client answer the phone, the scripted conversation might go something like this:

> [System Prompt: confirm that you are speaking to the right person]
> **Telemarketer:** *Is this John Doe?*
> **Resident:** *Yes.*
> [System Prompt: Inquire how the subject is doing; this generates emotional goodwill]
> **Telemarketer:** *How are you doing today?*
> **Resident:** *I'm doing good. Who is this?*
> [System Prompt: In a confident tone, let the subject know who you are and your intent in calling them and ask the qualifying question]
> **Telemarketer:** *This is Jane from ABC company, and I'm calling to set up a free one-hour financial consultation where we analyze your family's financial health. Is financial stability something that you'd like to find out more about?*

[System Prompt: Respond enthusiastically if the response is "Yes" and use Script 1. If the response is "indifference," use Script 2 with a tone of concern. If the response is no, respond with Script 3 with a tone of curiosity]

**Resident:** *I guess.*

[System Prompt: Script 2 – Ask the following questions to elicit more information. "How much have you thought about retirement? What is your retirement strategy? If you lost your job today, how many months of savings do you have available?"]

As the conversation progresses, the telemarketer vigilantly listens for keywords or key phrases that would prompt her to select a specific script.

**Resident:** *What do you mean by return on investment?*

[System Prompt: Use ROI Script]

**Telemarketer:** *Mr. Doe, that's a great question and a popular one. When it comes to generating a Return On Investment or ROI on your investment, a lot will depend on you. Many people don't like risk, so we guide them toward more conservative options. Other people have a high risk tolerance, so we guide them toward more aggressive options. Which category would you fall into? Conservative or aggressive?*

**Resident:** *I don't know?*

[System Prompt: If the subject answers conservative, use Script 1. If the subject answers aggressive, use Script 2. If the subject doesn't know, use Script 3]

**Telemarketer:** *Most people don't know. Which is why I'd like to go ahead and set up that free one-hour consultation.*

*Would Monday at 3pm work for you, or would Wednesday at 2 be better?*

As the telemarketer moves through the phone conversation, she needs to listen intently and simultaneously be able to call up the right mini-scripts and deliver the script with confidence, without losing the natural flow of the conversation. This isn't easy, especially for someone new to the task.

The profession of telemarketing isn't easy, and the churn rate (number of people quitting) is extremely high. Getting good salespeople to interrupt someone's day over the phone isn't easy. Rejection is high! The number of hang-ups or otherwise unreceptive clients will wear on just about anyone's psyche. Worse yet, training new telemarketers is a huge cost to the business, and even more significantly, the cost of an untrained or unseasoned telemarketer who might utter the wrong thing to a potential client is incalculable.

Depending on which study you choose to believe, the average tenure for a telemarketing employee is just over a year. The average churn rate varies, but the industry average hovers around 30%. The cost to replace one frontline person ranges from $6,000 to $16,000, depending on a variety of factors:

- Recruiting Cost: Cost incurred, directly incurred, or paid to a recruitment firm.

- Hiring Cost: Includes interviewing and processing a new employee.

- Training Cost: Both online and offline training on product, process, procedures, and soft-skill training.

- Coaching & Supervisory Cost: The amount of time a manager or colleague dedicates to training the new employee.

Assuming an annual churn rate of 30%, the costs can accumulate very quickly. A company with 100 employees will lose 30 employees per year. If we use an average annual cost of $10,000, that's $300,000 per year in unrecoverable costs without taking into account any opportunity costs[9] associated with a new hire.

The telemarketing industry has four major obstacles to profitability:

- Training Cost
- Telemarketer Inconsistency
- Churn Rate
- Sales Close Rate

**Call Me Back**

Here's where AI can play a key role in all four areas by using Voice Analysis technology. Imagine a telemarketer who knows exactly how the client is feeling on the other side of the phone. How would the telemarketer perform better if he was somehow advised of the client's shifts in mood (i.e., mood "dynamic"), during a phone interaction? How might this be possible?

*Sentiment Analysis* is the machine's ability to combine the acoustic characteristics of a customer's voice and the context of

---

[9] Opportunity cost is the cost of a foregone alternative. If you chose one alternative over another, then the cost of choosing that alternative is an opportunity cost. In this case, by choosing to invest in one employee over another who quits or is fired has a missed, albeit incalculable, opportunity cost associated with it.

the conversation into a simple score by which the customer's interest level may be determined. This is accomplished based on joint consideration of tone (i.e., spectral analysis), conversation velocity (words per minute), keywords, keyword phrases, and keyword frequency. In this manner, we gain some indications as to how the conversation was handled. Adding to this is a keyword cloud, where you can see which words were used most often, which may provide further indication as to the buyer's inclination.

The beauty of Machine Learning is its ability to take a constellation of data points and begin to predict or draw conclusions about the ideal buyer or telemarketer. This is not true causality of course, merely correlation, but the results can be compelling because high correlation often signals a causal relationship.

The trick is to pick the correct attributes. Luckily, one of the major advantages of Machine Learning in the Big Data milieu is to make this straightforward. In fact, many attributes can determine whether the potential client is a likely customer.

Our intelligent telemarketing system can then begin to collect information about the buyer in a highly directed manner. Gathered information might include:

- Intonation
- Stress in voice
- Change in stress (as a result of keywords or phrases used)
- Keywords used
- Word usage
- Speech velocity
- Time of day
- Male/Female

The machine can also collect similar data on the telemarketer side to help create a two-sided profile. Information on the buyer and telemarketer would be fed into the system along with whether the sale was successful or not.

Using predictive analytics, the machine would then be able to find patterns in the data to help optimize a desired outcome.

- Whether or not to call a client back.

- Determine what combination of keywords or phrases are more appealing to a client.

- Determine if it's important to match a client's voice velocity with a telemarketer's velocity.

- If the outcome is to determine what type of telemarketer you need to hire (male/female, age, tone, speech velocity, etc.)

- The efficacy of matching a telemarketer to client by race.

Let's say the desired outcome of using Machine Learning is to determine whether a client warrants a call back. Imagine the cost savings. If a telemarketer calls 100 people, talks to 10 and closes only 2 of the 10, that means 8 are in question. Do you call them back or not? Today, that's a judgment call.

What typically happens is that client is either put back into the queue (call pool) and called back within a given period of time (e.g., call back in 3 months), or the client is deleted from the database as a dead lead.

Let's assume that the lead is considered dead and is never "touched" again. That means for every telemarketer there are 8 dead leads per day. Multiply that by the number of working days in one year, 260, and that's 2,080 dead leads. Multiply that by 100, and you're looking at 20,800 leads. The question is what percentage of those supposedly dead leads are worth calling back.

For a human to perform this sifting and qualification task will require an up-front determination of whether or not the clients are worth calling back. Management would then need to develop some type of rule-based system to perform this function. In many cases, as I've mentioned, it's a subjective judgment call, which can wind up costing the company lots of money.

Could the work be done by human agents in an efficient and timely manner? That answer is most likely "no," and here is where Machine Learning can help. Machine Learning, specifically in the field of voice analytics, would not only automate this task but be able to recognize patterns that would otherwise be lost on the average telemarketer. This translates to higher efficiency and reduced cost.

**Speech-to-Text Transcription (STT)**

STT technology engenders a massive potential benefit to the sales world. It works in the following manner: When a consumer interacts with a human agent, the audio conversation is transcribed into text and stored as data. This information is then applied to Machine Learning and predictive analytics subsystems to identify a combination of consumer and agent speech patterns that signal possible intent. This is a powerful concept because the machine will then be able to perform a quick search to, for instance, determine what is the Next Best Action (NBA) when speaking with a client. It draws on data from past conversations, considers thousands of variables, and provides a script that is most likely to lead to a positive outcome. The possibilities are endless.

For example, if the client mentions she is moving to a new state and you have offices nearby that they can use, the machine is triggered by the words "office, Georgia" and will display a special offer that may be available at the new location. This technology is ideal for assessing and assisting in calls as they are taking place or afterward as part of a training exercise. The machine can also generate alerts based on keywords used during a conversation that a manager may want to review.

How does the machine know who is doing the talking when an agent and prospect are having a conversation? Well, this is a problem rather easily solved by a combination of digital signal processing (DSP) technology and smart computer algorithms.

Today's machines can perform a function called "Speaker Separation." During a phone conversation between prospect and agent, the call is recorded onto one audio channel. Speaker Separation then renders the conversation onto two separate audio channels, which can then be transcribed phonetically, indexed, and analyzed using sophisticated audio algorithms.

Even where there is "talk-over" (i.e., the agent and prospect speak at the same time), tailored digital signal processing algorithms can still detect and tease out the conversations separately and transcribe them.

**Sentiment Analysis**
What someone says is important, but the manner of delivery— that is, "how" it is said—can be far more significant. For example,

if I say the word "free," it may carry some information. But by emphatically stating the word "FREE" the system is able to detect, via pitch and tone, whether I'm stating it in the context of confusion ("Free? What do you mean free?"), excitement ("Free? Are you kidding me!"), or skepticism ("Free? Sounds like a scam!"). Succinctly put, speech attributes pertinent to emotions (Emotion Detection) are significant. Fortunately, emotion is correlated with distinct markers in vocal waveforms that can be rendered as Emotional Detection attributes (characteristics) that can be added to a customer database entry. Among other things, this information can be leveraged in the determination of whether or not a prospect warrants a call back.

Let's say we have 100 recorded calls of successful sales, and the objective (outcome) is to identify keywords used in these conversations that are more likely to influence a client to say "yes" rather than "no." The machine can generate a keyword cloud that sums up the frequency of usage of particular keywords or phrases associated with each response. Having this data gives the agent some insight into what his language selection should be when speaking to a potential client. For example, if the word "warranty" shows up often in a successful sales conversation, then the agent may be prompted to consider using the word and with a specified frequency.

Analyzing the data set further, we may also find that the keyword engenders a spatial (time) factor, indicating that when the keyword is introduced into a conversation significantly affects the outcome. For example, we may find that using the word "warranty" at a specified point in the conversation (e.g., within the first five minutes or during the last five minutes) is a high correlation factor in closing more sales.

This is a highly sophisticated effective analysis and derived sales tactic. Of course, we can go much further. The positive effects of a buzzword like "warranty" can extend to other keywords by measuring the efficacy of their correlation.

Now, by virtue of a simple logical extension, what if we needed to know *which* keyword to use, with *what* frequency, and in *what* context to have a successful sale? Could we do it? This might be a bit more challenging but still well within the realm of possibility. Of course, past a certain point, this concept might exceed normal human capability. However, machine language and predictive analytics as advisory tools can still provide a significant advantage in guiding us as to what to say, when to say it, and how to say it. It can process and analyze the data set far beyond human capability, generating optimally targeted suggestions so that a successful sale is rendered far more likely.

Here's a reasonable and practical scenario: After analyzing 100 phone logs of what prospects say over the phone, the machine is able to tell us through a keyword cloud representation which words correlate well with a successful sales call. We can then ask the machine to look other variables in the data set.

For example, we can ask the machine to look for words used before or after the word "interested" to see if we can find a phrase that correlates highly with a sale. The machine gives us the following phrases in which the keyword was used:

- Not interested (L)
- Not really interested (H)
- I'm interested (H)
- I have no interest right now (H)
- I'm not interested (L)
- No interest really (H)
- I'm hardly interested in (L)
- I may be interested (H)

- I have no real interest (L)
- Sound interesting (H)

We can then ask the machine to tell us which phrases are a better predictor of which prospects to call back. The machine may find that certain phrases, when used in the initial interaction with a prospect, have a high (H) correlation or a Low (L) correction with closing the sale.

The next level of filtering would be to ask the machine to analyze the audio files and detect the pitch, tone, or speech velocity (words per minute) used when the keyword or phrase was spoken. Here's where we see the real power of Machine Learning and its ability to use a multivariate approach to detect patterns that would otherwise be imperceptible to the average person.

Taking pitch, tone, and velocity into account, the machine is able to analyze the prospect's sentiment underlying the keyword "interested." It's worth mentioning the efficacy of this entire approach critically depends on the quality and sophistication of the audio signal processing algorithms used to detect phonemes, keywords, and key phrases.

The next step in the evolution of using these variables is integrating them into a more dynamic script. When precompiled scripts don't work, agents typically lack the power to change them or the know-how to adapt. Agents often aren't allowed to deviate from the script even in the event of consistent failure. This leads to substantial frustration and a poor attitude that inevitably "leaks," consciously or subconsciously, while talking to a prospect. A poor attitude begets a poor conversation, which begets a poor close rate. Now, that's causality or pretty close to it!

With Machine Learning, the aforementioned scripts can be modified dynamically. As the agent is talking to the prospect, a script pops up, based on the word usage of the prospect, instructing her to tactically adapt and always in the direction of the desired outcome.

The machine may tell her to use a key phrase, ask a key question, mention a specific feature, or introduce a new offer. The machine is listening, thinking, and advising the agent throughout the call. A virtuous cycle is thus created in which the machine guides the agent to a successful sale, the agent feels more confident, and this in turn leads to trust in the machine/advisor's capabilities. The impact on the churn rate and training time will undoubtedly be substantive and positive.

Takeaways:

- If the average telemarketer is making 100 calls per day and you have 100 employees, transcribing, analyzing, indexing and identifying patterns becomes a Herculean task.

- Using machine language also removes the subjective component of determining whether a prospect deserves a call back. Machine qualifying will increase the agent's close rate.

- The ability to identify keywords, keyword phrases along with timing in the conversation, tone, and speech velocity will allow you to incorporate these variables into script development with the goal of accelerating an agent's time-to-contribution (i.e., how fast they get up to speed and begin to sell effectively).

- Using better scripts will increase close rates. Furthermore, the agent's attitude is improved and stress-level reduced.

- When agents are more confident and successful, churn rates go down, thereby reducing a company's cost.

CHAPTER 3

# Data Analytics

*Processed data is becoming more valuable to companies as they use analytics to find new market segments that only Machine Learning can identify. Undiscovered markets (a.k.a. "Blue Ocean") may be a thing of the past in most cases, but undiscovered, small, revenue-rich markets (a.k.a. "Blue Puddles") are all around us.*

The world of data is growing at an unimaginable pace. More data has been created in the last 2 years than in the previous 100. Business leaders are beginning to understand the power of data and how they can leverage it in an era of little market differentiation.

Years ago, business leaders were talking about Blue Ocean[10] strategies: finding untapped markets with little or no competition. But even those oceans are now turning red with the bleeding profit margins of companies who are willing to lower their price to gain market share.

AI and Big Data present business leaders with a new paradigm to more easily target a given market segment, which I'll affectionately call "Blue Puddles." Contrast this with the complementary "Blue Ocean" strategies for finding new markets with big opportunities to sell volume or to a large customer base. Blue Puddles are small markets that have otherwise gone unnoticed by other companies. How can you find these Blue Puddles? AI is the short answer. Through its ability to analyze data and find new niche market opportunities or patterns in the data, companies will find incremental growth in their market segments.

Business leaders are now opening their minds and their corporate piggy banks to capitalize on opportunities created by large-scale data collection. This Big Data phenomenon is fueled in large part by relatively recent advancements in AI research combined with massively scaled, low-cost supercomputer processing and data storage.

Big Data + Sophisticated Algorithms + Low Cost of Storage + Computational Power = AI Growth

Companies are on the hunt for new market opportunities, new Blue Puddles. Armed with AI-enhanced insight, companies can now begin to formulate machine-driven business plans

---

[10] Blue Ocean Strategy is a marketing theory from a 2005 book by W. Chan Kim and Renée Mauborgne, professors at INSEAD and co-directors of the INSEAD Blue Ocean Strategy Institute.

providing what amounts to data-driven direction to wherever those opportunities might lie.

Here's the punchline: Winners in tomorrow's market will be those companies that deploy advanced analytics strategies in order to find untapped markets and then build a product or service set around that particular market.

Not having a data analytics strategy will handicap any company going forward. Companies who can identify and serve those aforementioned Blue Puddles first will see positive revenue growth.

On the other side of things, the Blue Ocean opportunities have become rare. In effect, they no longer exist unless created by a disrupting technology. Companies now face the option of being a market disruptor or aggregating Blue Puddles. The former comes with high risk and uncertainty of market success. Either is feasible, but the latter is a safer bet. Blue Puddle markets can be characterized based on:

1) A new market niche characterized by potential clients who are currently buying the company's core product offering

2) Being part of company's core offering

3) The possibility of an adjacent market

4) Revenue potential justifying a change in marketing strategy

5) Revenue potential justifying new product development

6) A market that is in its nascent stage

Under circumstances where such characterization is applicable, AI pattern recognition capabilities can be leveraged to find and serve markets before other companies catch on.

The drive to capture the power of analytics is being instigated in part by the emergence of the Internet of Things (IoT). More and more devices are now coming equipped with the ability to transmit data about the device and its usage. As the cost of production for products continue to drop and the efforts of miniaturization continue to increase, more and more products will be enabled to transmit data. As mentioned earlier, anything from thermostats to alarm clocks to your car will create data exhaust, and that exhaust is ubiquitous.

Much of this data is pertinent to business, and much of the "to do" concerning analytics centers on the need to capture, structure, store, and leverage this data as an asset. It will be useful at this juncture if we consider the fundamental nature of this IoT phenomenon a bit more closely, if for no other reason than to understand how it relates to our central topic (AI-based sales intelligence), and what critical trends might be expected from it.

The name "Internet-of-Things" is suggestive of what it actually is: a descriptive term referring to an Internet-based network of "things." Well, what are those things? We'll defer that question for a moment because once we understand how IoT functions, the "things" will become readily apparent in terms of a virtually infinite range of possibilities.

In many respects, IoT is simply the Internet taken to its obvious conclusion, whereby Internet itself becomes a transparent communications medium, much like old-style radio networks or microwave relay. Originally, the Internet was conceived as a medium for strictly human interaction as a means to facilitate data transfer among universities and laboratories. This later evolved into our present world of email, websites, search engines, and what have you.

However, as the underlying communications protocols became more sophisticated, yet another very smart person realized one could use this same communications infrastructure for data exchange among autonomous agents (i.e., specialized computer systems involving no direct human agency).

Furthermore, one could also leverage the communications protocols in such manner that ad hoc networks are created, still using the Internet as the basic medium but also secured against external traffic. This amounted to a new architectural paradigm for distribution of computer "smarts" to the actual physical locations where such resources are actually needed.

The immediate benefit to this is in savings of communications bandwidth (i.e., back-channel communications to some central location are effectively eliminated) and simplified hardware resource requirements (i.e., the demand for processing power and sophistication is determined by maximal requirements at any specific location as opposed to a global sum total).

The upshot of all this was the widespread appearance of smart-tech "boxes" consisting of specialized processors and, of course, the ubiquitous Internet interface. Once attached to the Internet infrastructure, these boxes are then connected to local data acquisition and control systems, thus constituting the Internet of Things.

These "boxes" are in fact the "things" referred to at the outset. They've made their appearance virtually everywhere— security, manufacturing, distribution, home networks, and much, much more.

In the present context, the significant consideration is that these IoT boxes are all talking to each other. Thus, we might consider high-level monitoring of IoT data traffic pertaining to "how much" stuff is being generated "where"; then "where," "who," and "how much" stuff is being consumed; and finally, among IoT systems, "who" is connected to "whom."

Now, in your mind, scale this across industries worldwide. This is the data-stuff analytics dreams are made of. Succinctly stated, IoT is already an important source for all things sales analytics, and if trends hold, this importance will only increase going forward.

Chris Mazzei, who is the Chief Analytics Officer at EY, said it best:

> In the past, there's been a distinction between the use of analytics to improve the current business processes versus the use of analytics to change the way the company is competing. Many companies started using analytics by focusing on processes, but as they saw success in this area, they realized it can help them in strategic ways, such as determining what to sell, how to sell it, whom to sell to, and how to stay differentiated from their competition. This gets to the fundamental role that advanced analytics can play in re-imagining the business. The ultimate role of advanced analytics is to help shape the fundamental business model for the next two years, five years, and beyond.

Companies are working to find ways to capture the data and turn it into a marketing advantage. The big question is, "How can companies use data and advanced analytics to identify markets and then act on that data to capture those myriad Blue Puddles?" In short, how can companies leverage the data and use it as a competitive differentiator? The ability to do so will drive the following business decisions and capabilities:

- Identify specific means to increase sales or revenues

- Inform investment decisions

- Aid in formulating a product development strategy

- Anticipate client needs

- Develop market tactical/strategic focus

Companies can be segmented into four categories or levels as to where they are with their analytics strategy:

Stage 4 – Leading: Analytics strategy is well established and central to the overall business strategy

Stage 3 – Challenging: Analytics strategy is established and starting to be viewed as a key strategic priority

Stage 2 – Developing: Analytics strategy is established for the enterprise, but not fully aligned across the business

Stage 1 – Lagging: Some analytics strategy exists for functions or lines of business OR no analytics vision or strategy extant at this time

Each stage comes with its own challenges. At the earliest stages, questions of budget and vision are most apparent. Does the company express a vision of how Big Data will transform its business, and is it willing to commit the financial resources to achieve that vision?

Another issue that rears its ugly head is getting buy-in from the C-Suite and stakeholders, who often are more focused on making a quick buck than investing in a long-term game, even with a high-confidence guarantee of a payoff.

As companies move to Stages 3 and 4, they may experience a scaling problem and a lack of collaboration with other departments or silos. Getting all a company's departments or profit centers to cooperate and collaborate in pulling data resources together and setting a common set of objectives is often difficult. Each department may be protective of its data fiefdom, and its desired outcome may differ from other departments.

The highest level of data analysis is necessarily fortified by a data-driven culture. Really, it's all about culture and the mindset that underpins it. What do we mean by this?

A data-driven culture is one that respects the process and rationale behind the data being collected, and of course, the actionable insights generated by the machine. Gut instincts and trends take second and third compared to what the data is indicating. "Shooting from the hip," as many are wont to do, is a serious "No-No" in the data-driven milieu. This is a difficult culture shift for many, particularly those traditionalists harking back to a bygone era.

Basing a long-term corporate strategy on data outputted from an AI algorithm requires a bit of faith. Yes, I see the logical irony in this statement. At a minimum, one must be willing to accept evidence possibly contrary to one's preconceived notions.

In any event, the proof is always in the pudding: an increasing number of companies are making serious profits based on this new data-driven paradigm. Here's what it takes to get it going:

- Commitment from top management and stakeholders

- Budget allocation

- Collaboration across departments

- Cultural acceptance of data analytics

- Organizational acceptance and restructuring

Here is but one component of the required paradigm-shift: Data is not an intangible asset or a thing to be treated with indifference. But rather, data is information expressing market trends and buying tendencies at ever-increasing levels of sophistication, and that represents a very tangible asset.

"Treating data as a strategic asset is as much a cultural change as putting the right capabilities in place," says Brenda Niehaus, Group CIO of Standard Bank. "You have to drive this from the highest levels of the organization and develop clear use cases so people can see, touch, and feel the value."[11]

For companies to begin leveraging the power and value of data, there has to be collaboration and cooperation across the organizational structure. Each department has to define what information it needs to achieve its strategic goals and then share those goals with other departments. They must also share the current information they have across silos, and a means to do this must be provided.

The more data the system has, the more value is expressed. AI has already demonstrated a fundamental truth: Data

---

[11]"Data & Advanced Analytics." *Forbes.* Jan. 24, 2017.
http://insights.forbes.com/advanced-analytics-high-stakes-high-rewards?aliId=271294436

has more value in aggregate than in individual silos. The challenge for data scientists within a company is to get different groups to create a common culture that relies on data-based decision-making for developing new products, finding new markets, and identifying new Blue Puddles to serve.

## Big Data

Since we're on the subject of data analytics, we may as well discuss the technology on which all the hype is based. Well, is it "hype" or is it "real"? After all, what is this analytics thing, anyway? What does the term really mean?

As with most things *hype*-ful, everyone seems to have their own definition and opinion. The situation today is somewhat reminiscent of the 1980s AI explosion. Few seem to remember or talk about it, but throughout this period, there were solid, worthy technical advances. However, the technology as it existed was being oversold. AI had become a buzzword, the very latest in high-tech fashion. Marketers—who for the most part had no idea what AI really entailed—were having a field day, dressed in glib words, slick presentations, and expensive suits. Customers were inevitably disappointed, and the technology took the fall.

As a cold reality dawned, corporate investment in AI research waned sharply. By 1995, no one was really working on it.

However, some 20 years have passed and what is old becomes new again. In the mid-2000s, someone figured out the new enterprise computer centers could be applied to processing Internet data on a massive scale and in an "AI-esque sort-of-way." Yet the current situation in AI is different from the '80s. We're now at one of those watershed moments, caught in the center of a perfect storm, a tipping point—Ray Kurzweil's "Singularity" if you will.

## Gaming the System

I'll give you two words why it is different now than it was then—well, two acronyms, one of which has become a word due to its ubiquitous presence touching the lives of every person on the planet: GPGPU and Internet.

Everyone knows what the "Internet" is and can attest to its power and presence. What's "GPGPU," then? It stands for General Purpose Computing on Graphics Processor.

It so happens that there exists in the computer world a radical subculture of gaming enthusiasts who have been pushing the computing performance envelope since Day One of personal computing. Their emphasis is different because they don't want to do databases, spreadsheets, or business accounting. Rather, they're interested in the most realistic graphics and raw speed, all in service of their gaming activities, of course.

Now, this group has incredible clout because they spend lots of "cost-is-no-object" money on their various toys, and here "bigger/faster" is most certainly "better." As a result, companies manufacturing powerful graphics hardware have been steadily upping their game to meet the demand and thus capture as much of this lucrative market sector as possible.

Around the mid-2000s, some brilliant person realized that the processing in these graphics units performed the same sort of generic matrix mathematics that supercomputers could do so well. In fact, all things considered, the Graphics Processing Units (GPUs) were faster and far more efficient. So this person's thought process must have been, "What if we write Applications Programming Interface (API) middleware that would make this untapped compute power accessible in a general programming environment?"

Thus, from this conceptual microcosm, the desktop supercomputer was born, and enterprise-scale GPU-accelerated supercomputing followed soon after. Now, of the top 10 supercomputers worldwide, *all* are GPU-accelerated.

GPGPU-accelerated supercomputers sound great, but what does that have to do with analytics? Well, lots when one considers Internet server farms, á là Google, can be similarly accelerated.

Analytics depends on data, generally massive amounts of it. And where does that come from? These days, that data is typically obtained via Internet!

When you do an Internet query (search), there's lots of unobserved processing behind those pages that show up in your browser. That processing can also be accelerated by GPGPU. The result is more data, and more data that's more salient to the original query. Furthermore, the analytics that is calculated based on the data you've thus acquired can now be processed on your multi-core GPGPU-accelerated workstation—something unheard of decades ago!

Again, what we're describing here is a perfect storm. We have the data, the computing power, and the problem (i.e., analytics). All the requisite pieces are in place. Where the nascent technology of AI is being considered, this is indeed a new situation.

So, what then is the connection between Big Data and AI? In our initial discussion of "What is AI," we mentioned a knowledge representation component. Among other aspects, this knowledge representation encodes logical relationships among some set of variables with assigned values.

Where do these data points come from? The Internet and Big Data. However, Internet and Big Data are not synonymous. One way of characterizing the difference is picturing "Internet" as the source and "Big Data" as a filter on that source.

A simple Internet query may return massive amounts of data, within which needed information is buried. Big Data then provides a means to extract that information in the form of *analytics* that can be directly used by the AI system.

Big Data processing can also be massive. A Big Data application is likely to be a front-end to the AI system, all running on your local workstation or distributed computing environment. The AI system will generate Internet queries (e.g., search for a particular client's interaction on social media channels), the result of which is preprocessed by the Big Data module and then fed to the AI system for "smart" processing on that generated analytics.

From a processing perspective, Big Data is highly diverse, spanning the parsing of documents for specific content, to image segmentation and object recognition, to pattern recognition in some abstract feature space.

For example, in the case of a possible sales lead opportunity, critical attributes might include market-sector value, market penetration, or purchasing trends. Pattern recognition employs these features as axes in a kind of mathematical space where, if we happen to have chosen the "right" features, the various things we want to identify occur as points within clearly defined clusters. Classification is then performed based on what cluster a given data point projected into this space is closest to. Thus, pattern recognition is reduced to a problem of simple geometry.

Of course, there are all sorts of hidden complexities. For example, Artificial Neural Network (ANN) classifiers, or Convolutional Neural Network (CNN) classifiers now all the rage, more or less obscure this geometric interpretation. However, this remains the basic idea.

For example, where a possible sales opportunity might be considered, pattern recognition may result in the classification of a sales lead as likely available in one product category or another based on a matched projection in feature-space. This is the stuff of analytics and the sort of information our AI system can leverage to advantage.

I hate to say it, but one of the reasons ANN and CNN constructs have become so popular is that they are very "cookbook" in application. That is, one doesn't have to know much about how things actually work.

For example, one may know virtually nothing about the inner workings of a particular client company. Rather, one simply looks at publicly available data for correlations as indicators of what that company might do. Useful data elements may include recent market activity, corporate structure, quarterly report, stock trends, and how they might be connected with other companies doing similar or perhaps complementary things. It all reduces to analytics of one form or another by which the AI system might extrapolate according to noted trends, correlations, and expressed patterns what said company might do. In the present context, this might mean when, what, and how much this company might buy.

However, nothing is known about the inner workings. The notion of extrapolation devoid of the internal contents might abrade purist scientific sensibilities, but this analytics methodology has proven extraordinarily powerful in practice. One simply can't argue with success.

## Monetization

The data being collected by companies will have an external value to clients in adjacent markets who may want to add to their knowledge base. Companies might then generate value based on the quality and quantity of data they gather. Among other things, this provides a larger incentive for top management to drive home the point that departmental silos must share data to obtain maximum value.

The demand for more data of ever-increasing quality and sophistication is skyrocketing as companies strive to more effectively learn about and address the needs of their customer base. Consequently, companies are willing to shell out hard cash for data sets that might aid in improving performance and finding new revenue streams.

The value proposition is obvious because the derived rewards in terms of revenue enhancement can be considerable. This has led to a new market sector in and of itself whereby companies that have implemented an effective monetization strategy based on Big Data expertise sell content and analytics know-how.

For companies that don't have such resources at hand, purchasing from an external source makes sense and may actually be an only option. As companies seek to get better insight into their customer base and market, advanced data analytics will become essential to effective strategic planning.

Leveraging data via analytics-derived insights will allow companies to:

- Sell data to new customers

- Combine company data and analytics with partners as a mechanism to leverage market position
- Sell analytics insights and analyses to new or existing clients

- Combine company data and analytics with partners to develop new products and services
- More easily identify data partners in the market

- Collaborate with complementary service providers

- Market and sell data to other companies for enhancement of the customer experience

Business leaders will be able to leverage data assets in a variety of ways to improve their view of the marketplace, better understand their customers, and search for untapped markets.

The key concept here is that better data enables a better decision-making process. For example, consider all the benefits that might be associated with the systematic adoption of data-driven analyses as the basis for new product development, service offerings, and justification for key decisions and investments.

Advanced analytics thus gives organizations a means to differentiate themselves from competitors and develop effective strategies for the evolution of products and services in the marketplace.

Takeaways:

- We're moving from Blue Ocean strategies to smaller, unnoticeable Blue Puddles for revenue growth opportunities.

- Big Data + Sophisticated Algorithms + Low Cost of Storage + Computational Power = AI Growth

- The Internet of Things (IoT) is powering Big Data.

- The algorithmic power of GPGPU in the gaming industry has now been applied to predictive analytics, generating new methodologies for uncovering insights.

- Companies need a collaborative AI strategy to remain competitive.

# CHAPTER 4

# Predictive Modeling

*Business leaders have been facing the cave wall watching the shadows of an Information Revolution that has shaped our decision-making process in the last couple of decades. We've reached the limits of spreadsheets and macros to help with our decision-making. Today, the ability to see the "angles" in a given market requires a higher order of intelligence just to navigate a highly commoditized business environment. Artificial intelligence, in the form of a new Predictive Modeling paradigm, is breaking the chains that bind, and only those leaders who choose to leave the cave and see the new reality will succeed in the decades to come.*

The power and use of artificial intelligence in business can take many forms, depending on what a company is attempting to achieve. In sales, the ability to predict "who will" and "who won't" is the single most powerful analytic tool a company can possess.

- Who will buy and who won't

- Who will cancel and who won't

- Who will renew and who won't

Unfortunately, predicting with certainty what a human being will do at a given time, when presented with a given option at a some given price, is impossible.

Prediction is all about probability or something close akin (e.g., "likelihood" or "confidence" that some given thing will happen). Machine Learning is about taking Big Data as input and building a Predictive Model that might be used to "score" the likelihood of something happening.

A Predictive Model generated from Machine Learning isn't an accurate science, but it's a great "guesstimator" as to who is "most likely" to make a favorable decision.

- Who will (most likely) buy and who won't

- Who will (most likely) cancel and who won't

- Who will (most likely) renew and who won't

In order to understand how Big Data, Machine Learning, and Predictive Models fit together, let's take a real-world example. First, let's zoom out once more and understand the basic components:

- Data: This is the information that is to be analyzed. Now, this information can come from different sources, but let's assume that we'll use a particular company's database to analyze the last five years of data. The number of variables and the time period it encompasses are often referred to as the data set. This is the INPUT.

- Machine Learning: This is a sophisticated algorithm developed by data scientists to analyze the data set (input) with the objective of finding patterns about "who will and who won't."

- Predictive Model: This is another algorithm that extrapolates (predicts) based on patterns detected by the Machine Learning component. Previously, this would have been a simple linear-regression or time-series model of a type you might find in an Excel spreadsheet. However, the mathematics is now far more sophisticated and has also been combined with a rule-based (AI) component, the sum total of which is far more effective in determining with high probability of success "who will and who won't." This is the OUTPUT.[12]

Now, let's look a common problem most companies have when trying to boost their revenues.[13] Say you have a database of 50,000 potential clients (contacts). The data set contains demographic information such as name, address, gender, marital status, age, and geographic location, and behavioral information such as visits to the website, page views, download requests, demo

---

[12] The visual I like use is that of a giant specialty filter. Those who can't get past it are the "will nots" and those that do pass are the "wills."

[13] In his book *Predictive Analytics*, which I highly recommend, Eric Siegel gives a great example on how marketing (and sales) can use modeling for an advertising campaign. I've taken his example and expanded on it to elaborate some of the subtleties of the application.

requests, newsletter signups, and search terms that have been used.

Marketing has decided to do a mail-out to this list that will hopefully prompt the contacts to go to the website and purchase a new product (Price = $500). Marketing estimates, based on past campaigns of this nature, indicate a response rate of 5%, which is deemed sufficient to justify the endeavor. Marketing then creates the flyer, uploads the contact database, presses the mail button, and sits back and waits for the results.

After a month, the results are in, and the numbers look like this:

COST

Cost of the mailer (postcard and postage) = $2/mailer

Number of contacts = 50,000

= Total cost of $100,000

Now, even though we've mailed out to 50,000 potential buyers, not all of them are actually going to buy. Marketing therefore has to guess what percentage will respond to the marketing effort, and this guessing drives the C-Suite nuts! It's hard to predict *who will* and *who won't*.

This scenario reminds me of John Wanamaker, an advertising pioneer who was quoted as saying, "Half the money I spend on advertising is wasted; the trouble is, I don't know which half." My modern version would be that "Marketing is part science and part hope; the problem is, I don't know which to depend on."

Now, a 3% response rate (i.e., the percentage of people who received the flyer, went to the website, and purchased the $500 item) would mean that 1,500 people bought.

REVENUE

1,500 People who responded x $500 Item Price = $750,000

In this world, our "sales" world, the bottom line is the only line that matters. If we calculate the profit by taking our total revenue and subtracting the total cost,[14] we get:

PROFIT = $750,000 – $100,000 = $650,000

Based on these results, the marketing campaign is judged as a success by the company, and everyone is happy. Marketing breathes a sigh of relief that although their response rate was estimated at 5%, a 3% still represents a win. Now, any rational business leader, after viewing this successful campaign, will ask four basic questions:

1.    Can we do it again?

2.    Will it be just as successful?

3.    Can we improve the results?

4.    If so, by how much?

Marketing will respond to the first question with a vigorous "yes we can." After all, they'd like to remain relevant and thus keep their jobs.

To the second question, "Will it be as successful?", they may feel good about what they've already done and respond in the affirmative.

---

[14] For the sake of simplicity only the cost of the mailer itself is used. In the real world, there are obviously general and administrative costs associated with this marketing campaign that should be accounted for in order to get a better approximation of the true cost.

To the question of, "Can we improve the results?", they may offer up ideas like, "If we improve the layout of the flyer, change the colors or fonts, and time the mail-out, we may be able to improve the results."

To the final question, "If so, by how much?", they may have to make a "finger-in-the-wind" guess since their 5% prediction was off by 2%—quite a sizeable error.

This is how marketing has always operated: a series of campaigns with some successes and some failures, of course with hopefully more of the former and fewer of the latter. The key point is this all-too-typical marketing methodology is error-laden and inherently unpredictable.

It's now time for marketing to turn to Machine Learning to help improve the success rate and predictability of marketing campaigns.

Let's assume that marketing takes their customer data set, along with historical results of their various marketing campaigns, and feeds that information (INPUT) into their Machine Learning Platform, which will produce a Predictive Model on *who will* and *who won't* (OUTPUT).

Marketing now takes their list of 50,000 potential clients and runs it through their Predictive Model. The model then spits out a list of ONLY 3,000 who are "more likely to buy."

COST

3,000 x $2/mailer = $6,000

REVENUE

3,000 x $500 Item Price = $1,500,000

PROFIT

$1,500,000 – $6,000 = $1,494,000

Let's pause for a moment and analyze the profitability of this campaign. These numbers show 100% of the contacts buying; this isn't reality. The model is giving us a select group of clients, based on the data set, who are "more likely to buy than not." This means that our response rate will be higher compared to doing a mail-out to the entire list. But it does NOT mean that 100% will buy. The model is predicting the likelihood, not guaranteeing it.

A more realistic prediction may be that people on this list are "X-times more likely to buy than not." Let's assume that among those in this "highly likely" data set, we find that 2,000 actually buy. Our numbers are then as follows:

### COST
3,000 x $2/mailer = $6,000

### REVENUE
2,000 x $500 Item Price = $1,000,000

### PROFIT
$1,500,000 – $6,000 = $994,000

Let's take a moment to compare the two campaigns; without and with a Predictive Model. We can see a 100% increase in Revenue, but we see a dramatic drop in risk on the Cost side. The latter is what will really drive the growth of Predictive Modeling.

| Revenue | Cost | Profit |
|---|---|---|
| $750,000 | $100,000 | $650,000 |

| $1,500,000 | $6,000 | $994,000 |
|---|---|---|
| 100% | -94% | +53% |

Companies are looking for ways to compete more effectively, which means they have to be more discerning about where they invest their marketing dollars. Using a Predictive Model allows them to *reduce their exposure* to marketing campaigns that historically have more misses than hits. In one recent survey, companies turning to artificial intelligence as means to create a profit wedge[15] in their business model are seeing an "8.1x" increase in revenue and an "8.4x" decrease in cost.

Digging a little deeper into what a Predictive Model looks like, let's create an oversimplified version for illustrative purposes, if only to appreciate the enormous task Machine Language undertakes.

Many different models can be used to predict what someone will do given a certain set of variables. Let's imagine that the aforementioned database expresses variables derived from the following content categories: demographics and online behavior, the latter drawn from the company's web analytics. Machine Learning would produce a linear model that may look something like this:

| Demographic Variable | Scoring |
|---|---|
| Male | 11.3 |

---

[15] A profit wedge is when a company increases its top line and simultaneously drives down its cost (i.e., they drive a wedge between the revenue line and cost line).

| | |
|---|---|
| Female | 14.1 |
| Age Range (25–45) | 10.7 |
| Marital Status | 22.0 |
| Military | 21.0 |
| Geographic Location | 5.0 |
| Income Level | 15.9 |
| **Online Variable** | **Scoring** |
| Search Term (Keywords) | 17.1 |
| Newsletter Request | 7.5 |
| Demo Request | 25.5 |
| Download Whitepaper | 17.3 |
| # of Website Visits (greater than X) | 5.0 |
| Page Views (greater than X) | 10.0 |
| Browser | 5.5 |
| Company Email | 10.0 |
| Free Email (Yahoo, Hotmail, Gmail, etc.) | 2.1 |

Based on the data it has and past results of various marketing campaigns, the Machine has assigned each variable a "score" (i.e., the higher the score, the higher the correlation of "will buy"). The

Predictive Model would use a rule-based model to sort through the "will or will not" buyers using the simple heuristics (rules of thumb).

In this example, anyone above the scores listed, or some combination thereof, would be considered "highly likely to buy."

Rule 1: If the Demographic score is above 79.9

Rule 2: If the Online score is above 63.5

Rule 3: If the Demographic score is above 54.3 AND the Online score is above 45.2

If these are existing clients, we can use historical data to generate more clarity about their willingness to buy.

| Past Purchase Variable | Scoring |
|---|---|
| Bought X Product | 17.1 |
| Bought in the Last 90 Days | 12.5 |
| Order Size (greater than X) | 15.5 |
| Buyer Title: Purchasing, Buyer | 12.3 |
| Bought with Credit Card | 10.0 |
| Used Payment Terms | 15.0 |
| Picked Up Purchase | 5.5 |
| Frequency of Purchases in the Last 90 Days | 10.0 |
| Annual Revenues (from credit application) | 2.1 |

Now the Predictive Model starts to get a bit more complex.

Rule 1: If the Demographic score is above 79.9

Rule 2: If the Online score is above 63.5

Rule 3: If the Demographic score is above 54.3
AND the Online score is above 45.2

Rule 4: If the Past Purchase score is above 75

Rule 5: If the Demographic score is above 54.3
AND the Online score is above 45.2
AND the Past Purchase score is above 63

Rule 6: If the Demographic score is above 54.3
OR the Online score is above 45.2
AND the Past Purchase score is above 63

I could add a few more permutations, but you get the idea. In this example, we are only working with 3 sources (i.e., demographic variables, social variables, and past history variables). Now imagine if we added a fourth database? A fifth? You immediately understand that for a mere mortal, keeping track of all the permutations becomes a logistical (rules) and mathematical (scoring) nightmare.

As we add more data sources, Machine Learning is able to take this information and reformulate a new Predictive Model with supervised learning (i.e., the results are applied as a feedback input to the machine, and corrective rules or actions are taken). Note that, in the present context, the "supervised" in "supervised learning" implies human agency in selecting and applying a given predictive output generated by the machine, then collecting an observed result, and then applying that result as feedback to the machine.

With this feedback mechanism in place, the Machine Learning component generates over successive iterations a series of model instances, each of which is a more accurate predictor than the previous. One might then ask, "Will this model converge to a point where not much correction is required?" The answer is "Yes." If our machine is of sufficient power and sophistication, we'll soon arrive at a model we can trust, until the market changes. At that point, the learning process begins anew. Given that markets are always dynamic, a safe bet is that both "we" and "the machine" must keep learning.

The concept of *Deep Learning* comes into play when the machine autonomously seeks unrealized structure in the data and then develops Predictive Models based on any new relationships or patterns it might find. These algorithmic refinements are not programmed or hard-coded by any human agent; these are increasingly complex algorithms that the machine formulates on its own.

Think back to when you were learning to ride a bike. You had training wheels to stabilize your bike and a parent to provide the right nudge (left or right) and a push to keep you going. After a while, the parent would let go, and you rode the bike on your own. Later you learned how to "pop" the front wheel up and ride the bike that way. Or, if you're more adventurous, you learned how to stand on the seat and ride with no hands. At this point, your parent is no longer teaching you; you're improvising new "moves" and learning on your own. This is a very loose description of Deep Learning, but you get the gist.

By construction, the machine is learning to be "creative" in finding new associations and relationships in the data to provide actionable insight you didn't see, or perhaps you observed the raw data but couldn't comprehend its deeper meaning.

What are some applications that we can use in selling more effectively in this hypercompetitive market? Well, we know that client retention is more of a predictor of business stability than client acquisition. In other words, keeping clients buying from us is a more certain way to grow the business as compared to attempting to acquire new clients. With that in mind, here are some concrete applications of how Deep Learning can help us retain clients:

- Cancellation: What if we could predict ahead of time the likelihood of a client canceling? If we had this list of potential cancellations ahead of time, we could embark on some type of customer reinvigoration campaign. We would call the client and do a free, one-hour consultation to answer any questions they might have, or we would schedule an onsite visit to uncover and address any problems or concerns.

- Renewal: If a client is up for renewal, which clients need to be contacted to ensure they follow through? Let's say we are leasing broadband services to a large B2B company, and we want them to renew instead of opting for a competitor. The machine would alert us about which clients are at risk of not renewing, and the salesperson would then reach out with a renewal discount or other customer appreciation incentive.

- Upsell or Cross-Sell: What if the machine could predict which clients are ready to either upgrade their product or service (upsell), or consider buying another product or service (cross-sell) the company offers? The customer wins because they are being offered something they need (but didn't ask for), or hadn't considered that another product might help them run their business more effectively. This is a so-called *preemptive* sales approach that, if done correctly, adds value to the customer experience.

Predictive modeling gives companies the anticipatory power to take actions necessary to gain or keep their customer's business. Here is a short list of actions companies can take to retain, upsell, or cross-sell an existing customer:

- Give the customer a call (i.e., the "personal" touch)

- Offer a discount to show appreciation for their past business

- Send an email to touch base

- Send an offer via electronic newsletter

- Recommend a product they may be interested in

- Offer a free onsite review of how they're using the products they've purchased

- Send an invitation to a free webinar

- Schedule a lunch-and-learn

- Have upper management call the customer to express their appreciation

- Send the customer a small gift (e.g., a shirt with your company's logo)

- Invite the customer onsite to meet the staff

- Send them free tickets to an upcoming event

The list can go on, and I'm sure you can add a few suggestions of your own. The key point is that through Predictive Modeling, we can improve our chances of retaining clients by becoming more aware of those who might choose to take their business elsewhere.

In other words, Predictive Modeling sheds a light on those dark corners of our database where customers can get lost. The implied advantages are huge. In fact, if current trends hold (as they surely will), this technology will be essential in acquiring or maintaining a competitive advantage. Using Machine Learning to grow your business is not a matter of "if," but "when."

When I hear skeptical managers dismiss Predictive Modeling or Machine Learning as technology outliers, I'm reminded of Plato's Allegory of the Cave. Plato describes a group of people who have lived their entire lives chained in a cave, facing a blank wall. The prisoners watch the shadows projected on the wall from objects passing in front of a fire behind them. These shadows are their only reality, the only world they know. One day, some prisoners in the cave manage to break free and leave the cave only to discover that their reality, shadows on the wall, was not at all what they thought it was.

Those business leaders of a more "traditional" mindset have been facing the cave wall, watching the shadows of the

Information Revolution. This is what has shaped their various decision-making processes in recent decades. However, contrary to what they might believe, they've already reached the limits of spreadsheets and macros as an aid to their decision-making.

Today, the ability to see the "angles" in any given market requires a higher order of intelligence to navigate, among other factors, a highly commoditized business environment. Artificial intelligence, in the form of a "smart" Predictive Modeling capability, is breaking the chains that bind, and only those leaders who choose to leave the cave and see the new reality will succeed in the decades to come.

Takeaways:

- We can use Predictive Modeling to serve existing clients better.

- Using different data sources, we are able to predict which clients may choose to take their business elsewhere.

- Using Predictive Models, companies can reduce their cost exposure by spending only on prospects more likely to buy than not.

- Decision-makers have to embrace the new algorithms if they want to stay competitive in the market.

# PART 2: AI APPLICATIONS

# CHAPTER 5

# Sales & Singularity

*Let an ultra-intelligent machine be defined as a machine that can far surpass all the intellectual activities of any man however clever. Since the design of machines is one of these intellectual activities, an ultra-intelligent machine could design even better machines; there would then unquestionably be an "intelligence explosion," and the intelligence of man would be left far behind.*

I.J. Goode

When will a machine be able to match or excel human cognition? When will a machine be able to think for itself and apply creativity to problems that haven't been learned or programmed by a human? When will the machine transcend the binary world of 1 and 0s and appear more human than humans?

Given present context, these are all reasonable questions. Furthermore, any answer one might provide short of "never" would then mark a threshold of *Singularity*—when the machine can think for itself, solve problems for itself, and perhaps even eventually be able to run its own empathy algorithm.

The British mathematician Alan Turing, often considered the father of modern computer science, believed that machines would one day be able to do what humans do and more. In 1950, Turing published an article entitled "Computing Machinery and Intelligence," where he introduced a simple test that could be used to confirm whether a machine's intelligence had crossed the threshold of Singularity. The so-called Turing Test is a simple interrogative construct that involves three parties: a human, a computer, and a human interrogator.

The test is set up as a blind test; think Pepsi versus Coca-Cola. A computer (A) and a human (B) are placed behind a barrier. The human interrogator (C) is on the other side of that barrier.

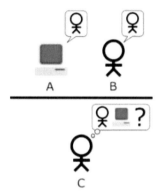

**Figure 3: Turing Test (Source: SingularitySymposium.com)**

The interrogator will ask questions via keyboard and will see the responses from A and B on a computer screen. The interrogator must determine if the answer was generated by the computer or a human. If the interrogator is unable to guess accurately whether the human or computer answered, the computer is considered intelligent. In other words, if you can ask a human or computer (machine) a complex question and you're unable to distinguish which agent (computer or human) might have answered the question, it's fair to conclude the machine has achieved a level of sophistication tantamount to an intelligence, the difference of which is imperceptible to an average human (an interrogator).

This is an interesting and subtle idea, but one with an obvious flaw. To wit, what happens when the machine is far more intelligent than a human? How do we then rank or score such an outcome? It goes without saying such a circumstance is far beyond anything possible today. However, scientists worldwide agree the possibility is real.

That which lies beyond mere intelligence within a machine is what brings us to the concept of "Singularity," and although the British mathematician I.J. Goode did not use the word singularity, he did describe what this singularity would look like. Following his work with Turing, Goode wrote,

> Let an ultra-intelligent machine be defined as a machine that can far surpass all the intellectual activities of any man however clever. Since the design of machines is one of these intellectual activities, an ultra-intelligent machine could design even better machines; there would then unquestionably be an "intelligence explosion," and the intelligence of man would be left far behind.

Arguably, Goode is describing the emergence of Deep Learning technology, the result of which is being observed in today's marketplaces. Have we reached the point of Singularity?

Ray Kurzweil, Google's Director of Engineering and world-renowned futurist, predicts that this technological

Singularity will happen sometime in the next 30 years. Kurzweil states:

> 2029 is the consistent date I have predicted for when an AI will pass a valid Turing test and therefore achieve human levels of intelligence. I have set the date 2045 for the "Singularity" which is when we will multiply our effective intelligence a billion fold by merging with the intelligence we have created.[16]

Whether or not you agree with this date, a Singularity of some form will happen with very high confidence. It's simply just a matter of when. Many don't believe the timeframe is as soon as Kurtzweil suggests. The folks over at Singularity Hub did their own informal survey on Twitter, and the results are a bit scattered, as you might expect.

**Figure 4: Singularity Hub Survey**

---

[16] Galeon, Dom and Christianna Reedy. "Kurzweil Claims that the Singularity Will Happen by 2045." *Futurism.* October 5, 2017. https://futurism.com/kurzweil-claims-that-the-singularity-will-happen-by-2045/

Whatever the timeframe, the questions that concern the average individual are of a more practical, down-to-earth nature: "How will artificial intelligence affect our lives? How will it change how or where we work? What does it mean for the next generation?"

The immediate reaction by many is to assume that Machine Learning will take away their jobs. Many have visions of a dystopian future with machines running the world and humans scrounging about under their cybernetic boot. That's a bit dramatic and, dare I say, reactionary.

The truth of all these futuristic musings is likely a bit less dramatic but still exciting nonetheless. Whether we've noticed it or not, we've entered into the Fourth Industrial Revolution.[17] The changes have already begun. The "rise of the machine" is real in the sense that a new capability to aid us in doing what we do has emerged. This capability will restructure our economic system and the means by which we make decisions in virtually every aspect of our lives. Here's just a smidge of historical perspective:

- First Industrial Revolution: Use of water and steam power to mechanize productions (e.g., powered looms), which displaced artisans. The Luddites[18] destroyed the looms as a form of protest against progress.

---

[17] The World Economic Forum declared that in 2016 humanity had entered into the Fourth Industrial Revolution.

[18] Workers in England (1811–16) who organized to destroy manufacturing machinery, under the belief that its use diminished employment. The term Luddite is used to describe anyone who is opposed or resistant to new technologies or technological change.

- Second Industrial Revolution: Machines displaced human labor and assembly lines, and mass production displaced skilled laborers.

- Third Industrial Revolution: Electronics and information technology were used to automate production even further and displace laborers.

- Fourth Industrial Revolution: Machine Learning will displace both intellectual and unskilled jobs.

Some claim the Fourth Revolution brings with it something that previous revolutions had not—the convergence of human and machine as one.

In the previous revolutions, the change in technology stood "outside" as something other than oneself. The promise of an impending Singularity means that human and machine will, to at least some extent, merge. Without a doubt, the tools of this Fourth Industrial Revolution provide the means to infringe on the privacy of individual and if taken to the extreme, the sovereignty of the individual.

Klaus Schwab, founder and Executive Chairman of the World Economic Forum, captured the anxiety of how people feel about Machine Learning:

> Now a Fourth Industrial Revolution is building on the Third, the digital revolution that has been occurring since the middle of the last century. It is characterized by a

fusion of technologies that is blurring the lines between the physical, digital, and biological spheres.[19]

I suppose that means we have an interesting future ahead of us. As with all "revolutions," humanity will have to choose how best to live and prosper.

## Displacement, Not Replacement

The biggest concern for the average individual may be, "What will that mean for my job in the future? How will this impact me?" It goes without saying that with every revolution, there are casualties, and this revolution will be no different.

Oxford University predicted that by 2025, 47% of jobs will, to some extent, be automated.[20] To put that number in perspective, there are approximately 155 million jobs in the U.S., and approximately 72.8 million of those jobs will be automated. That number seems a bit high, particularly in the given timeframe.

What's lacking is a bit of clarification and granularity about the term "automated." "Automated" doesn't necessarily imply "replaced." We also need to understand what is intended when we say a given "job is automated" because the phrase is both contextual and subject to interpretation.

Consider the fact any job is defined in terms of a list of tasks. A salesperson doesn't just sell; he must perform a defined list of tasks so as to ensure success. Some of these tasks involve

---

[19] Schwab, Klaus. "The Fourth Industrial Revolution: what it means, how to respond." World Economic Forum.

[20] Frey, Carl Benedikt & Michael A. Osborne. "The Future of Employment: How Susceptible Are Jobs to Computerization?" University of Oxford, 2013. http://www.oxfordmartin.ox.ac.uk/downloads/academic/The_Future_of_Empl oyment.pdf

going out and getting new business or maintaining existing business while other tasks require ancillary activities directly or indirectly in support of the sale function.

In a complex B2B type of sale, the salesperson may have to perform the following tasks:

- Sort through new leads
- Prioritize leads
- Cold call leads
- Send follow-up emails
- Respond to general inquiries via phone or online
- Call existing clients to keep in touch
- Deal with client emergencies or problems
- Generate a weekly report
- Set up customer meetings
- Travel to visit a customer
- Make plane, hotel, and car reservations
- Collect receipts
- Fill out expense reports
- Update the CRM
- Prepare customer presentations
- Develop a customized proposal
- Call clients for clarification
- Proposal check and cross-check
- RFM analysis[21]
- Generate and submit proposal pricing

---

[21] An RFM analysis looks at the buying history of a customer. You want to look at three factors: Recency – How recently a customer has made a purchase; Frequency – How often a customer makes a purchase; and Monetary Value – How much money a customer spends on purchases. If history is any indication of future behavior, this will give you some perspective on the customer's buying motivation.

- Proposal follow-up
- Ask for the order
- Submit contract
- Negotiate aspects of the contract
- Acquire final approval from legal
- Acquire the necessary signatures
- Close the sale

If you're in sales, you can either expand on this list or remove a few items. The point is that the "job of selling" is more like a list of tasks or actions that the salesperson must do, in aggregate, to fulfill total requirements for her job function.

One might then reasonably ask, "Can a machine replace every task or aspect of this sales process?" The answer is probably not, at least not in the near future. So the question becomes: Which of the listed tasks can be automated, and which are likely to remain as part of the salesperson's duties?

Now, let's revisit the Oxford study that stated that 47% of jobs will be automated. It may be more appropriate to view that number as a "finger-in-the-wind" metric since each job, with its varying task, will be automated differently.

Returning to the B2B sales example, I've now crossed out those tasks that today can be handled by a machine. You can see that a human is still needed to make a cold call and follow up just to keep in touch. If there is an emergency outside the normal, that also is something only a human can handle.

- ~~Sort through new leads~~
- ~~Prioritize leads~~
- Cold call leads
- ~~Send follow-up emails~~
- ~~Respond to general inquiries via phone or online~~

- Call existing clients to keep in touch
- Deal with client emergency or problem
- ~~Generate a weekly report~~
- ~~Set up customer meetings~~
- Travel to visit a customer
- ~~Make plane, hotel, and car reservations~~
- Collect receipts
- Fill out expense reports
- Update the CRM
- Prepare customer presentations
- ~~Develop a customized proposal~~
- Call client for clarification
- Check that all items are included in the proposal
- ~~RFM analysis~~
- ~~Submit proposal pricing~~
- Follow-up on the proposal
- Ask for the order
- Submit contract
- Negotiate aspects of the contract
- Get final approval from legal
- Get the necessary signatures
- Close the sale

Again, if you're in the selling game, Machine Learning could be a great thing as we'll explore in the later chapters. One of the most significant advantages of artificial intelligence is its handling of many of the rote or mundane tasks associated with selling. My "finger-in-the-wind" metric tells me that in the near future, some 30% of our tasks as salespeople will be automated. That's a good thing in terms of optimizing sales performance because we'll then have more time for those things the machine cannot yet do.

As we look toward the AI horizon, any given job will be impacted in one of three ways. The first one we've already touched on: task automation, which will enable salespeople to improve the customer experience, mainly by virtue of the salesperson being more available.

The second AI impact will be job replacement. For example, instead of having 20 people working at a telecenter, a virtual assistant will be able to greatly facilitate handling of inbound calls.

Lastly, there is job displacement. Often viewed as a negative, I instead view job displacement as a shift toward the positive side of the learning and growth curve for individuals. Wealth creation is not a zero-sum game where one's win equals another's loss. The creation of new tools in AI may also create new opportunities in other areas of the business that will allow an individual to learn, grow, and achieve a higher level of success.

In the sales domain, the vaunted Singularity remains distant. This isn't necessarily true for other domains, but that's another story. Here, we are concerned with sales, and for the foreseeable future, the profession of selling is still safe—depending on what you're selling.

I see susceptibility for replacement in sales on a sliding scale between commodity and complexity. For salespeople who are selling a commodity product or service, you may find yourself displaced more quickly than those selling more complex items.

Takeaways:

- When a computer can behave cognitively like a human, we will have reached a point of Singularity.

- The Fourth Industrial Revolution centers around Machine Learning displacing both intellectual and unskilled jobs.

- Every job should be viewed as a list of tasks, and not all tasks can be automated.

- Automating tasks frees up the salesperson to either hunt for more business or better serve existing clients.

# CHAPTER 6

# Salesforce.com

*Today's buyers are going online to educate themselves on what they want to buy. They will search and sift through information until they are ready to either buy or reach out to the vendor for more information that might push them over the "buy line." The singular advantage is, of course, the customer has already articulated a need. In effect, the Internet has shifted the role of marketing into the selling space, which means marketing professionals have a greater role to play in increasing a company's sales velocity.*

In the late '90s, software was being packaged and sold to customers at a high price, and any type of maintenance, installation, or customization accrued as an add-on cost. Then, in March 1999, Marc Benioff, Parker Harris, Frank Dominguez, and Dave Moellenhoff began to work on a software platform entitled Customer Relationship Management (CRM).

A CRM software system allows the user to store and manage client or prospect information (e.g., contact information, interactions, track sales by clients, track sales opportunities, etc.). The goal was to sell the software over the Internet instead of normal distribution channels as an off-the-shelf package containing installation discs, a bookcase full of manuals, and what have you. This CRM system represented a new way of looking at the customer maintenance problem in that it was geared to directly support the salesperson's interaction with clients and the methodological conventions the salesperson might employ during the selling process.

For example, instead of putting your client information onto a spreadsheet (e.g., Excel) known to be difficult to track, manage, maintain, and reliably disseminate, a far more sophisticated user interface was offered. The CRM system is also secured as an enterprise asset and centralized on a common database, improving access and information sharing.

In comparison, a spreadsheet is viable for only a small number of clients. You can easily create rows for each client and columns to represent each step of the sales process. Every time you interact with a client, you can add notes to each respective row. However, at the level of 25, 50, 100, or even more clients, usability becomes overwhelmingly cumbersome. This is an architectural scaling issue that CRM solves quite handily.

In simplest terms, CRM allows salespeople to easily manage a customer contact, track progress, and share with others in the organization. The result is the successful closing of more deals and increased customer loyalty via a thorough and consistent engagement.

One of the most significant of CRM's advantages is the ability for anyone in the company to have access and view the corresponding interactions across your salesforce. For example, if a client calls with an emergency and the salesperson assigned to the account in unavailable, anyone on the team can pull up the client's purchasing history and any relevant conversations between the client and salesperson. At this point, the person handling the emergency call can then take all necessary actions required to solve the problem. Once resolved, that person will then update the CRM. Later, when the salesperson does become available, he will receive an alert along with notes on the emergency and how it was handled. The salesperson can then follow up with the client to make sure the emergency was handled to their satisfaction.

This CRM platform also eliminated the traditional need of having to develop, distribute, install, and maintain a custom software-program-plus-database onto a computer. As an aside, this new model of selling an application in the form of an enterprise corporate-wide resource facilitated a shift in thinking toward "no software." CRM actually is software, but of a ubiquitous sort by construction. It is intended to solve all software needs as an Internet-based subscription service in one go. Thus, it becomes effectively "transparent" (i.e., no software).

Pursuing this theme a bit further, it's interesting to note for historical purposes that the original CRM software was modeled after Amazon's easy-to-navigate site with a minimalist look—simple tabs across the top.[22]

---

[22] Notice the first line in graphic: "Account Sign-up Bonus: Get a complimentary Zig Ziglar tape when you open a SalesForce account by June 30, 1999." Zig Ziglar was a sales and motivational speaker who influenced and motivated, and still motivates, many of the world's best salespeople. I'd thought I'd highlight this for any Ziglar fans out there.

**Figure 5: Early Saleforce.com Interface**

As Salesforce entered the new millennium, companies selling into already-saturated markets realized they somehow had to differentiate themselves. It was around this time in 2000 the "no software" mantra was coined, later becoming synonymous with Salesforce.com. This "small" company was in fact making a "large" statement that would be the harbinger of things to come in how software would be delivered.

The old model of developing software was giving way to a subscription platform that would avoid many of the costs and pitfalls that other software companies faced. By moving to a subscription model, the company no longer had to worry about how many versions of their software were installed on computers.

In 2003, with momentum building, Salesforce decided to hold its first annual conference, "Dreamforce," where the company would be able to meet with their "Dreamforcers" (i.e., diehard believers). The goal of the event was to demonstrate the latest bells and whistles of the platform and, more importantly, network with users and representatives on what could be done to make the platform more robust.

The first Dreamforce was held in downtown San Francisco with over 1,000 registered attendees. Dreamforce was used to showcase and launch Sforce 2.0, the industry's first on-demand application service.

Not content with being a normal platform provider, in 2005 Salesforce developed a service called AppExchange that disrupted their software space again. This new service allowed developers to develop their own CRM applications; all Salesforce customers could then invest in and develop applications that fit their particular model.

What Steve Jobs did for the iPhone, Salesforce did for the companies who wanted to develop a specific application to enhance the platform into what they wanted. By 2006, Dreamforce had grown to more than 5,000 tribe members who would gather to celebrate the company's growth, find out about new applications, and hear from industry experts from other market segments.

---

Small Business CRM from Salesforce

Even if your customer base is small, no one can keep every interaction — ones that have happened, or need to happen — memorized and organized.

At Salesforce, we believe small businesses can use technology as a force multiplier to punch way above their weight. Our cloud-based CRM solution levels the playing field for your small business.

Because Salesforce is in the cloud, it can grow and scale with your business. You can easily add features from tons of apps in our marketplaces without adding costly infrastructure, and

Salesforce upgrades are instantly implemented as soon as they're available without disruption. With all your information on customers, prospects, and leads stored on a single online platform, everyone in your business has access to the latest information — no more version control headaches or out-of-date spreadsheets. Need to ensure your salespeople have access to the information they need when out at customer meetings? No problem. Our CRM system is fully mobile, so your data is available on any connected device, at any time.

On average, Salesforce helps our customers boost their sales by 37%. But the benefits of Salesforce CRM for small business don't end when you make a sale. Customer Service benefits, too. Our solutions help to build stronger relationships with your current customers, win new ones, and accelerate business growth. And intelligent marketing automation helps you focus resources on the tasks that really add value, while a common platform for all your data helps to build strong relationships across all your channels, including social, Web, email, and customer call centers.

Source: Salesforce.com

Salesforce eventually added Visualforce, a tool that allowed users to create their own Graphical User Interface (GUI). The bridge from Software-as-a-Service to Platform-as-a-Service was complete. Companies or third-party developers were able to build applications customized for their particular business model using the horsepower and architectural functionality available at Salesforce.com.

Over the years, Salesforce has continued to grow its platform and its capabilities and continually focuses on developing tools for its customer base.

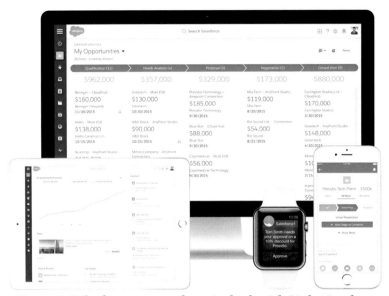

**Figure 6: Salesforce.com updates its look with Lightning but still keeping its "Tab" style**

Leap forward to 2016, and Salesforce's investment in computing power and algorithmic sophistication is now manifested in Einstein—Salesforce's official step into the world of AI.

Einstein allows companies to use existing AI tools and algorithms to uncover actionable insights into their customers' buying behaviors. These insights can then be leveraged to optimize how a company serves its customers. Better servicing the customer is about increasing revenue while optimizing business practices internally is about reducing inefficiencies (costs). The totality creates a so-called *profit wedge* by which companies might enjoy an increased success in the marketplace.

When Salesforce announced Einstein at their Dreamforce annual event, there were more than 170,000 present to witness this significant moment that was 17 years in the making.

## Einstein Spreads the Love

With annual revenues climbing toward $10B dollars, Marc Benioff (CEO) and his team have a come a long way in building this behemoth that has now become the standard when any CRM is mentioned.

Einstein will now make artificial intelligence available to a broader scope of clients. The ability to use Machine Learning algorithms and Deep Learning will allow companies to extract insights that could change the course of their business.

The ability to intelligently manage a client database represents the next wave in prospecting, customer engagement, and selling in general. Einstein today is the only CRM using AI to improve the quality of information available to sales representatives, who'll be able to anticipate and predict customer behavior in all aspects of the sales process.

Einstein comes "data-ready," which means there is no preparation of the data needed. This is a critical advantage because any global rehashing of unstructured data is by definition a time-consuming chore. In the present context, unstructured data consists of information "chunks" that must first be interpreted and formatted just so a database can accept it. Einstein is different in this respect because it is not architecturally bound to the strictures of a traditional database.

Armed as it is with AI "smarts," Einstein readily accepts and processes unstructured data in a manner more or less transparent to the user. Once the data is inputted, Einstein then applies a host of algorithms that sort and extract key insights to customer behavioral patterns, the results of which can then be used to launch new products or services, or perhaps identify new markets worthy of attention.

The question remaining is exactly how this is done—the means by which Einstein acquires and structures data that isn't structured. This is of interest because in the Internet Age, lots of potentially important data occurs in an unstructured form. Examples include social media postings, images, web search history, press releases, and more. Succinctly put, we want to take advantage of these information resources.

Let's take the example of a target client who has posted something on LinkedIn. How might that information be structured and thus rendered usable for the Machine?

**The Value Lead**

Every lead that comes to your company has a value associated with it that is derived by analyzing the behavior of the lead or the source of the lead. A lead behavior value can be calculated based on how much interaction you've had with the lead via your company's website, chatbot, or direct dialogue via phone. In simplest terms, the more a lead engages with your company, the higher the assigned value.

Think about it: If someone wants to really buy from you, they will download the information they need from your website, ask questions via the chatbot, and maybe call just to hear it from the proverbial horse's mouth. These are signature behaviors of a person who is interested in buying your product or engaging your service.

A lead that comes from a valid reference or source will also be assigned a high value. For example, if someone recommended your company and the lead reached out, the lead is then assigned a high lead value. In sales we know that referrals falling into these categories close much easier and faster than cold leads (i.e., those that just "happened upon" our site).

Another example is if the lead came from a list (database) of clients who've purchased similar products from other vendors. That lead might be assigned a high value since they fall into the company's target market.

Finally, inactive leads are also assigned a high value. A client who hasn't bought in the last 6–12 months still might be a good candidate to reach out to.

In a perfect world, a salesperson should be able to manage and track all aspects of this value scoring system. The reality is that the time constraints put on salespeople to sell often puts them in a position where their ability to tag and manage clients and track interactions becomes a seriously daunting task.

In fact, the task is simply not scalable. At a certain number of clients, it becomes overwhelmingly complex and thus impossible to perform correctly. Typical manifestations of the problem include a salesperson routinely grabbing at the first lead that might come across her desk, or in an equally desperate maneuver, reflexively sifting through hundreds and in some cases thousands of leads, and then making what amounts to an ill-informed, low-probability-of-success judgment call on which specific leads to follow up on.

Carrying this line of thought a bit further, two problems are thus revealed: (1) quality of information and (2) complexity of the task itself. Imperfect or limited information hinders the salesperson's ability to make good decisions, and the problem is dramatically worsened as the number of leads increases. This is where the scalability issue comes to the fore.

Here's a reality we all must face: The human brain can only manage so much before it is forced to rely on instinct and intuition as a failsafe default. Intuition and instinct were prized abilities back in the day when globalization and the Internet were distant, yet-to-be-imagined realities. They still are. However, in today's hypercompetitive market, the salesperson must also become a "rational agent" in his approach to any given market. This includes determining who gets his attention, and in what order.

The implication here is that the instinct and intuition that have served us so well are no longer sufficient. Given the burgeoning demands of the task, the modern salesperson needs AI to augment his sales ability.

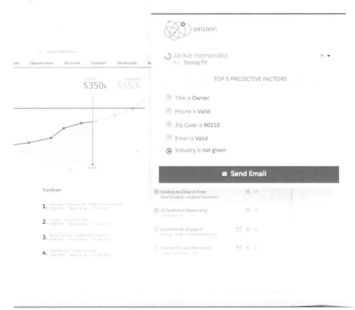

**Figure 7: See new leads, lead scores, and the factors behind lead the scores.**

This is where Salesforce's Einstein will help optimize the day-to-day activities of salespeople. Einstein will be the salesperson's rational agent, sifting through the long list of potential clients to uncover those who are more likely to buy and thus prioritize a "hit list."

Using some form of lead scoring algorithm similar to the one previously described, Einstein will analyze the lead's engagement behavior, reviewing historical sales data and any other relevant data sets to determine whether the lead is likely to convert into a potential sale AND whether they are likely to do it now or in the future.

Einstein might automatically discover, based on your latest data in Salesforce, that VPs in a certain industry who view demos are great leads. In fact, it not only discovers the insight, but it predicts just how likely the lead will be to convert with a smart lead score. Einstein even provides direct insight into how the score was determined automatically.[23]

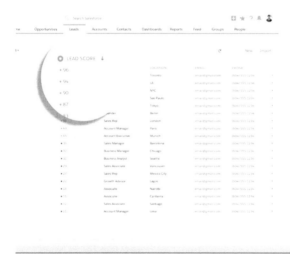

**Figure 8: Prioritize leads based on their lead score, quickly and easily.**

---

[23] Salesforce.com. "Einstein Lead Scoring." Predictive-Lead-Scoring.pdf

As Einstein collects more data, it will improve the quality of its algorithm using supervised Machine Learning. Remember, the form of Machine Learning we're assuming requires supervision whereas the ideal algorithm does not; an unsupervised learning algorithm is what every company aspires to. However, we not at that point just yet.

Thus, with the assumed supervised Machine Learning in place, Salesforce's data scientists will analyze and review outcomes generated from potential sales and lost sales to determine what went right and wrong, and subsequently feed that information back into Einstein as a corrective input.

For example, if all the buying signals or factors in Einstein point to a high probability of a sale, and the deal doesn't go through, then the data scientists have to step in and analyze what went wrong. The data scientist will then review massive amounts of data and use the information to adjust or teach Einstein to be "smarter and more discerning" when it predicts which leads should be contacted and in what order. This is in itself a complex task. However, the underlying mathematics is robust and well established. Therefore, in practice, the training methodology is rendered relatively straightforward.

This iterative cycle of corrective reinforcement, aided by the data scientist's input and adjustments over time, teaches the machine. This is what mathematicians call a "convergent process." That is, the machine's learning state approaches a constant value at which no further corrections are required, unless of course the problem (market) changes. The ultimate goal is a point where supervision of any form is no longer required. This is actually much closer than we might think.

Unsupervised Machine Learning already exists as a practical reality, and substantive advancements are being made every day. At some point in the not-too-distant-future, our AI-enhanced CRM won't require any training intervention at all from the data scientists (human agents).

However, this won't change much for the salespeople who might be involved as human agents still make the final decisions as to "what to do" in any given situation. Rather, the real task will be for this new unsupervised CRM to "explain" itself—express a rationale in arriving at a given suggestion, ranking, or some other output.

---

**How Einstein Lead Scoring Works**

Einstein Lead Scoring models are built specifically for each customer and organization, which ensures that the models are tailored to the business. How? Einstein Lead Scoring analyzes all standard and custom fields attached to the Lead object, then tries different Predictive Models such as Logistic Regression, Random Forests, and Naïve Bayes. It automatically selects the best one based on a sample dataset. There is no need for a PhD in statistical analysis or mathematics because Sales Cloud Einstein has done the heavy lifting by finding the best model to drive lead conversion. Instanced models are updated monthly to make sure you have the most accurate predictions for your leads. Leads are scored every hour using the latest model. If something changes on one of your leads, it will be rescored within the next hour.

**Top Benefits**
- Increased connection and conversion rates
- Accelerated engagement with the best leads
- Improved understanding of lead score factors

---

**Top Features**
- Zero Setup — No implementation overhead or import/export to separate tools
- Custom Lead Score Data-Driven Workflows — Easily assign tasks based on predictive lead scores
- Smart Lead Lists — Surface the best leads quickly

source: salesforce.com, "Einstein Lead Scoring"

**Sales Optimization**

If you're following the conversation thus far, it will be apparent Einstein's impact on a given company's salesforce is potentially quite substantial. Among other things, it will automate all the low-level or mundane tasks for a salesperson, in principle freeing them to more closely focus on sales behaviors critical to engaging with clients or closing a deal. The results are salespeople who are generally more productive and clients who are benefitting from an enhanced customer experience (i.e., salespeople and customer service offering useful insights and actionable suggestions).

Accenture's Chief Technology Officer, Paul Daugherty says it best:

> [AI] frees up employees to do things they get more satisfaction out of, which is solving more complex problems, and dealing with the more complex issues that arise in business. The technology can learn the workers' capability, help them understand best practice and help workers do higher-skilled jobs with higher quality, higher productivity, more effectively.

The study "Artificial Intelligence is the Future of Growth" drives home how AI will create growth by automating simple or mundane tasks across a broad cross-section of industries, markets, and roles. Daugherty firmly believes that AI is the greatest transformative force to our global economy today.

> We're just at the start of a new era of applying artificial intelligence in a big way to transform business… It will be bigger than the cloud, it will be bigger than the overall digital business wave we're looking at because it stands to transform the way humans interact with technology and its consumers and workers.[24]

Of course, the challenges faced by salespeople today will vary depending on the specific industry, market and customer base being considered. That being said, many salespeople are struggling with:

- Administrative tasks that don't affect their sales directly— filling out expense reports, coordinating meeting schedules, responding to low-priority questions from low-probability leads, generating weekly reports for management, and so on.

- Sifting through leads collected from a multiplicity of sources (e.g., trade shows, social media, websites, cold calling, etc.) and deciding which leads to call on first (i.e., prioritizing as a basis for a contact strategy).

---

[24] Purdy, Mark and Paul Daugherty. "Why Artificial Intelligence is the Future of Growth." https://www.accenture.com/us-en/_acnmedia/PDF-33/Accenture-Why-AI-is-the-Future-of-Growth.pdf

- Client research and creation of customized presentations based on their company's current needs as well as matching the client with the right product or service.
- Creating proposals for clients who may be looking for a complex solution or who require options in their pricing.

- Pulling together next month's or next quarter's forecast and being able to predict with a high level of certainty where their number will be. Forecasts are important because they drive resource allocation of time, effort, and raw material in a production scenario.

Einstein will enable salespeople to manage these challenges far more efficiently and with far less investment of time on the salesperson's part. For example, instead of a salesperson having to sift through the week's activities to generate a weekly report, Einstein would be able to do that with a few clicks of the mouse.

And what if Einstein could provide you with some insights into why certain activities (e.g., lost deals) happened? For example, with each weekly report, the salesperson is required to pull together all sales activities and discuss deals that were either lost or simply "continued" into the next quarter or budget cycle. The salesperson is then left to explain "what happened" and unassisted may only be able to provide anecdotal support for why a deal was lost or delayed. Here's where Einstein may be able to lend a hand.

Any Machine Learning algorithms employed within this sales milieu would be assigned to scour different data sources to uncover new or relevant information that may impact current or future sales. Einstein would be able to insert some "clippings" from different online sources on those companies where the deal was stalled (put on hold) or lost. The salesperson is then able to review this information and include it as part of the issued report. This will help the salesperson better understand what's going on in her market and also help her explain to upper management the relevant specifics of a stalled or lost deal. This is but one example of how artificial intelligence can help salespeople be more effective at developing an understanding of their market and aligning priorities with prospective clients who are deemed more likely to buy than not.

> *Often people only think of AI boosting growth by substituting humans, but actually huge value is going to come from the new goods, services, and innovations AI will enable.*
>
> David Autor, Professor of Economics, MIT

**Square Business**

According to a recent report by the McKinsey Global Institute,[25] adoption of artificial intelligence will impact many sectors such as retail, education, manufacturing and so on. Considering retail sales in particular, companies developing and deploying an AI strategy might see the following results:

- 65% potential reduction in lost sales due to product unavailability

---

[25] "Artificial Intelligence: The Next Digital Frontier?" McKinsey Global Institute (MGI), 2017. MGI-Artificial-Intelligence-Discussion-paper.pdf

- 30% increase in online sales with dynamic pricing and personalization

- 2 million fewer product returns per year with more accurate demand forecasting

Square is a company that is already leveraging the power of Salesforce's intelligent CRM. In their own words,

> Square enables sellers to accept card payments and also provides enhanced services including reporting and analytics, next-day settlement, and chargeback protection. Square's point-of-sale software and other business services help sellers manage inventory, locations, and employees, access financing; engage customers; and grow sales. Square Cash is an easy way for businesses and individuals to send and receive money.

Square is using Salesforce Einstein within the Sales Cloud to provide real-time predictive analysis for leads. At the Dreamforce 2016 annual event, Taylor Cascino—then Head of Sales at Square—spoke about how they planned to use Einstein to generate insights into captured leads, scoring each of them and then updating sales personnel in a summary report about which of those leads exhibit the highest potential. His latest comment speaks volumes to the success Square is experiencing with use of this technology: "Square scores 25K leads per month and realized a 64% year-over-year increase in revenue."

The AI sales formula used by many companies will follow a basic pattern:

1. Collect data on leads from various sources.

2.  Analyze the data using a variety of algorithms.

3.  Use Predictive Analytics to produce actionable insights and/or recognize unseen patterns.

4.  Prioritize what leads need to be followed up on.

5.  Generate any additional insights, via a dashboard, that will allow the salesperson to modify his presentations to or conversations with a sales lead so as to enhance the customer experience.

Without a doubt, AI-based systems such as Salesforce's Einstein will continue to positively impact many areas of the selling game, and all of this comes down to the salesperson's enhanced ability to sell more effectively.

Takeaways:

- Salesforce.com is a CRM system that can help manage your client database more effectively.

- With the advancements of AI, applications or platforms like Einstein will help salespeople in choosing which leads to pursue.

- Lead scoring is and will continue to be an evolving science.

- The better we are able to score leads, the better we can forecast demand.

CHAPTER 7

# Sherlocking
# Social Media

*The biggest misperception about IBM Watson is that it's meant to replace humans. Watson works with humans to enhance the abilities of professionals at every level, from highly specialized surgeons to oil drillers, and automates many basic tasks. However, no matter how advanced the technology, some jobs—specifically, those that rely heavily on empathy, ethical judgment, and social interaction—will always be performed better by humans.*

*Cognitive computing introduces a new level of collaboration between man and machine. It will augment and expand human intelligence, not replace it.*

*IBM Vice President Ed Harbour, IBM Watson Project*

Every second, around 6,000 tweets are published on Twitter, which corresponds to over 350,000 tweets sent per minute, 500 million tweets per day and around 200 billion tweets per year. Worldwide, there are over 2.01 billion monthly active Facebook users, 1.15 billion of whom are mobile and active daily and 1.32 billion people on average who log onto Facebook. On YouTube, 300 hours of videos are uploaded every minute with 4,950,000,000 video views per day. The total number of hours of video watched on YouTube each month is 3.25 billion hours. These numbers are both staggering and overwhelming.

All this information being generated every day reminds me of the silly story about two boys who were told to clean out a grain silo filled with horse manure and that whatever they found, they could keep. After some time, the first boy emerged from the silo disgusted and dirtied and wanted no part of that experience again. The second boy emerged dirtied as well but with a huge grin on his face. When asked why he was smiling, he responded, "It's dirty, but I'm sure there's a horse in there somewhere."

When I view the social media dataverse from a business perspective, I feel like the second boy. "There's a lot of crap out there, but I know there's some valuable data in there somewhere." The emergent question is how one might extract that data and turn it into a usable and executable information resource that might help businesses to grow.

As salespeople, we are faced with the daunting task of finding new customers or new markets in which we might sell our products and services. There was a time, pre-Internet, where growing a company's revenue was more about pounding the pavement and hustling for new business.

Today, with an enhanced access to information, clients are smarter, have more knowledge, and thus have more options, making it much more difficult for salespeople to locate and capture new opportunities. Even when an opportunity is identified, a challenge still remains in determining if that client is too far along into the buying cycle or perhaps not far enough along to make a decision.

Traditionally, the only way to tell if a client is ready is to call, set up an appointment, schedule a meeting, and hope that that timing favors you. However, the sad reality, given the intense nature of current markets, is the salesperson often doesn't have the time or luxury to pursue every opportunity to this degree. The new challenge then is to find the right customer with the right message and the right product offering, and all at the right time. Timing is becoming the critical variable in determining a salesperson's success in the market.

Touch the client too early, and they aren't ready to make a buying decision. Touch them too late, and they've already narrowed their choices (i.e., their preferences have been formed) to a shortlist where you unfortunately didn't make the cut.

The answer to "better timing" in prospecting for new business may lie in our ability to extract information and actionable insight from the varying social media platforms.

The questions then are, Can we actually use that data from our social media platforms in order to find new opportunities? What if we knew based on social data which clients to pursue and which to let go? How might such a thing be done? It again comes down to identifying some means to predict when a buyer is ready to make a buying decision.

## Suite Feelings

"Elementary, my dear Watson" is a phrase often attributed to Sherlock Holmes, the English detective in the works of Sir Arthur

Conan Doyle. In the movie version, Sherlock Holmes utters this phrase when he is ready to explain his reasoning in solving a crime. Based on evidence, observed behavior, and clues, Holmes can deduce what really happened and thus solve the crime. His companion Watson is always present as a catalyst, assisting Holmes in solving the mystery.

Likewise, IBM Watson will be a catalyst in helping salespeople solve the mystery of identifying the right buyers at the right time. Watson IBM is an AI-driven platform that uses predictive analytics and sophisticated algorithms to find patterns, connections, and similarities (correlations) in the data that will help identify potential markets and buyers.

The Watson supercomputer processes at a rate of 80 teraflops (trillion floating-point operations per second). This "teraflops" is computer-ese term useful for characterizing a computer's raw processing capability. Just know that "80 TFLOPS," as they're called, represents *lots* of processing power, well into the supercomputer range. In any event, to replicate (or surpass) a high-functioning human's ability to answer questions, Watson accesses some 90 servers with a combined data storage capacity of over 200 million pages of information, which it then processes against six million logic rules. Just to establish scale, the device and its data are self-contained in a space that could accommodate some 10 refrigerators.[26]

The power to take data and transform it into actionable insight with Watson has been made available for companies to use. In fact, companies can now leverage the power of this supercomputer for a small monthly fee.

---

[26] Rouse, Margaret. "What is IBM Watson supercomputer? - Definition from WhatIs.com." WhatIs.com. June 2016.
http://whatis.techtarget.com/definition/IBM-Watson-supercomputer.

Here's a rough outline of how Watson can be used and how sales and marketing can leverage their existing data sets:

1. Upload your social media data

2. Define the keywords you want the machine to capture

3. Categorize these keywords into situational uses

4. Run an analysis with various algorithms (analytics)

5. Visualize the data in different forms or representations

6. Locate associations

7. Dive deep into associations

8. Extract possible content (insights)

9. Develop an action plan

10. Measure the results

IBM Watson can now pull information from your own company's social media activity, as well as the dataverse in general, and then generate analytics-based attributes, including sentiment (mood), emotion (feeling) and tone (communication). This level of information will allow the machine to assess client intent. Based on what a client says and how she might say it, we can now datamine these social conversations and make a determination as to where the client is in the buying cycle.

In 2015 IBM acquired Alchemy API,[27] whose technology is now a core component of the cognitive APIs (Application Program Interfaces) offered on IBM's Watson Developer Cloud. With these new social media monitoring tools, clients can now develop their own specific applications for their marketing and communication departments. Companies are now able to easily analyze a client's mood and needs from afar and determine a next course of action.

No longer do salespeople need to meet with a client to get a sense of what he might be thinking. Instead, Alchemy's APIs can be applied to the analysis of a target client's online communications or posts as a far more robust source for this type of information. Arguably, this will be as close to a true "crystal ball" as you're likely to get.

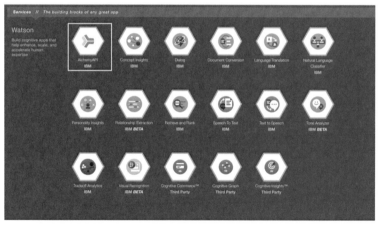

**Figure 9: IBM Watson Suite with AlchemyAPI**

AlchemyLanguage is a suite of Natural Language Processing (NLP) tools that can help you understand text but more importantly, assess "meaning" behind that text. The text in

---

[27] More information can be found at http://www.AlchemyAPI.com.

question might come from your company's Twitter feeds, postings on LinkedIn, articles on your website, press releases, and so on.

Once collected, all this information can be analyzed and processed to produce key insights. For example, the algorithm can identify keyword(s) that you want to monitor. If you're in sales, you may want to monitor any feed or document that contains a phrase related to your industry. If you're in the telecommunications sector, you may want to monitor for words like "fiber optics," "broadband," "wireless" and so on. Along with keyword extraction, the algorithm can also do entity extraction where you can detect if companies or people are also mentioned in that text.

Consider a situation where you, the salesperson, are assigned a portfolio of key accounts, and your job is to find a way to get in and meet with the key influencers in hopes of nabbing the first sale. AlchemyLanguage or something like it is your secret weapon. You instruct the machine to be on the lookout for specific keywords but more importantly, any mention of key influencers or decision-makers contextually associated with those keywords.

In a manner similar to Google Alert, you'll be notified when the keyword(s) you've selected are detected online. Any appearance of keywords will also trigger deeper contextual analyses that might also result in identification of key influencers who might be directly approached with a sales pitch. Note that the NLP algorithm contextual analysis is sophisticated in that it understands text syntax and semantics. Thus, if your company happens to be named Orange, it will respond to instances of "Orange the company" and not "Orange the fruit."

Keyword detection alone doesn't exhaust the full capabilities of tools such as AlchemyLanguage NLP suite. Users and developers will also be able to perform Sentiment Analysis to classify text as positive, negative, or neutral. The fact that it performs this analysis at the document level implies anything from a published article to a Twitter post represents a valid input.

From a reputation standpoint, you could monitor for any mention of your company's name using the entity extraction feature and then determine what sentiment is being associated with your company's name. You can monitor for what others like or dislike about your company or other types of associations. For companies wanting to protect their brand online, NLP represents an important technological advance as it will allow companies to detect and respond to any negative press being pushed out into the dataverse. Or, if the sentiment is positive, NLP can provide contextual information about pertinent actions to further leverage that momentum.

This might sound trite or self-absorbed, but being able to monitor what others are saying about you, your products, or your company is critical in today's market. Given that consumers and buyers are constantly searching online for new products or service, being able to respond appropriately to any attempt to smear the company or brand is more important than ever.

**Tell Me How You Really Feel**

In its simplest form, Sentiment Analysis quantifies the mood of a tweet or comment by counting the number of positive and negative words. That is, by adding or subtracting the negative and positive scores, a sentiment score is generated by the machine. Let's say your company ABC launched a new product, and it has been shipping for two weeks. Marketing will want to monitor any feedback on social media as a means to gauge market receptivity.

The AI platform will then be instructed to monitor any mentions of ABC or the product (we'll call it a Gizmo). Once a post (document) is found, keyword extraction is performed, and a sentiment score will be generated. Here's an oversimplified example to demonstrate the basic idea:

Post: *I really like ABC's new Gizmo. It's easy to use and set up was fast. #VeryCool*

Keyword Extraction:
ABC
Gizmo
Like
Easy
Fast
VeryCool

Sentiment Analysis:
Like = +1
Easy = +1
Fast = +1
VeryCool = +1

Sentiment Score: +4

As an actionable insight, marketing should capitalize on this positive score by promoting how easy it is to use the Gizmo. They may want to launch a new video campaign online or buy online advertisement touting the "coolness" of the Gizmo. Or, you can simply share this post as part of the social media campaign.

As part of the Sentiment Analysis, you could also correlate the positive keywords extracted with the number of likes, retweets, or shares of the posting. For example, you may find that when the word "cool" is used, the post is clicked on more often and is more likely to be "liked" or shared. This will trigger marketing to create posts of the new product incorporating the word "cool" in different variations.

A neutral post on social media really doesn't provide a company with any polarized information. An innocuous post may look something like this:

Post: *Just got my new Gizmo. Time to test it out. #Gizmo*

> Keyword Extraction:
> Gizmo
> Received
> Test

> Sentiment Analysis:
> Got = 0
> Time = 0
> Test = 0

> Sentiment Score: 0

A negative posting of your new product launch could look something like this:

Post: *Received my Gizmo from ABC. Box damaged. Long setup time. What a nightmare. #NotCool*

> Keyword Extraction:
> Received
> Gizmo
> ABC
> Damaged
> (long) Setup Time

Nightmare

(Not) Cool

Sentiment Analysis:

Received = +1

Damaged = −1

(Long) Setup Time = −1

Nightmare = −1

(Not) Easy = −1

(Not) Cool = −1

Sentiment Score: −4 (+1 − 5)

In this example, words that would normally be considered either neutral (e.g., setup time) or positive (e.g., easy and cool) are now given a negative score because of the negative adjective (long) and negative adverb (not) used in describing the product or the customer experience. A post with this low of a score could trigger the machine to generate an alert for marketing to act on. The first question marketing needs to ask themselves is, "Is this an isolated incident?" If so, marketing should route this post to an internal sales rep or customer service agent and reach out to the user on social media and attempt to resolve the issue. Others who may come across this post will see how fast the company is moving to assist and resolve the issue. The hope is that this case is an isolated incident and can be resolved quickly to minimize any negative impressions online.

Analyzing one post and resolving the issue is easy to do and can be done by human hands. But what happens when you have to analyze thousands of posts where the sentiments of the consumers are more scattered and obscured?

This is where Machine Learning steps in and perhaps discovers that online post statistics for cumulative Sentiment Scores are skewing negative. The machine will then generate an alert along with a report highlighting what keywords are trending negative.

For example, if the keyword "damaged" or semantic variations thereof (e.g., damage, broken, dented, crushed) appear with high frequency, a problem in the company's shipping process may be indicated. Thus forewarned, an immediate corrective action may then be initiated.

There are many useful variations on the Sentiment Scoring theme. For example, from a B2B large-account sales perspective, the last thing you want is a target client to be speaking negatively about your product online. This is effectively a public venue, and any such comments might prove highly damaging. If such comments are detected, an alert can be sent to the appropriate company representative, who can then move quickly to reach out to the customer and resolve outstanding issues.

The process of reducing an opinion to a number isn't a perfect science, and a data scientist will still need to conduct supervised learning to improve the machine's algorithm. For example, one area of improvement for NLP may be an ability to understand or correctly interpret sarcasm. The machine may have a hard time distinguishing a positive comment from a sarcastic remark.

Post: *Love my new Gizmo. Yeah, right! #ILoveTorture*

Arguably, this example is a bit hyperbolic and might well represent a statistical outlier. However, the point remains. In this particular case, a bit more training might be required. But as time goes on, these little language quirks can usually be resolved.

# Trump's Tweets

During the election campaign of 2016, much discussion revolved around who was sending out Donald Trump's tweets. A number of articles described how the tone of Trump's tweets is more positive when they come from an iPhone device than when they come from an Android. The hypothesis is that Trump tweets from an Android device and that he employs social media assistants who tweet from an iPhone. But how do you work that out?

You add the sentiment scores to a data set, and then compare the sentiment scores for the different devices. You can try this example out for yourself in Displayr.

In a data set containing 1,512 tweets from @realDonaldTrump sent during the primaries, there is a small but positive average sentiment score of 0.3, with scores ranging from –5 to 6. This means that the average tweet has slightly more positive language than negative. The magnitude of the scores is small as the length of a tweet is restricted.

The power of sentiment arises when considering other variables present in the data. Think of the now-famous example of the Trump sentiment gap between Android and iPhone. The mean sentiment score of tweets from Android, 0.1, is significantly lower than the overall average of 0.3:

| Average | Twitter for Android | Twitter for iPhone | NET |
|---|---|---|---|
| Sentiment | .1 ↓ | .5 ↑ | .3 |

Sentiment by Source of Tweets
sample size = 1512; 95% confidence level

If these mean scores don't sway you, then you may find the shape of the distribution more convincing:

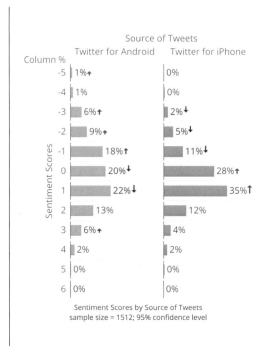

Sentiment Scores by Source of Tweets
sample size = 1512; 95% confidence level

The iPhone has a greater proportion of neutral (0) and slightly positive (1) tweets. The Android has fewer such tweets, and a greater proportion of tweets with a negative score.

Source: Displayr is a data science, visualization, and reporting platform. See webpage at https://www.displayr.com/sentiment-analysis-simple/

**Figure 10: Displayr**

### I Feel You

Another tool in the AlchemyLanguage suite that can be used to dig deeper into Sentiment Analysis is the Emotional Analysis API, which can uncover yet another layer of our online communications. Understanding the emotion that people associate with your product or company gives you more information about your company's image.

Sentiment Analysis classifies text for positive, negative, or neutral language. An Emotional Analysis is based on probability along five emotional axes:

1. Joy
2. Anger
3. Disgust
4. Fear
5. Sadness

When you paste your text or document into the API, the analysis will yield a probability for each of the five dimensions. Now, as part of the training process, the Machine Learning algorithm has been fed a large number of conversational examples (e.g., tweets, postings, articles, etc.) on different uses of sentiment in language. When the text is analyzed, the algorithm pulls from what it has "learned" and will assign the text or document a score along these five emotions.

Now, let's go analyze an article concerning Trump's tweets as an example of how the Displayr tool can be used to detect emotion or bias. We begin by first *defining a desired outcome* in terms of type of output. What do we want to extract from this article? What information do we seek? For example, let's say that we want to know:

1. Does this article speak poorly of Trump?
2. Is the author a fan of an Android or iPhone?

By simply copying and pasting the article into the Emotional Analyzer and clicking the "analyze" button, we will obtain an analysis output in seconds. The results for each of the five emotions will range from 0.0 to 1.0. In this example, a score >

0.5 indicates strong emotion along that particular dimension (Anger, Disgust, Fear, Joy, and Sadness). Here are the results:

| Entity | Relevance | Sentiment | Type |
| --- | --- | --- | --- |
| Donald Trump | 0.804867 | positive | Person |

| Emotion | Score |
| --- | --- |
| Anger | 0.095557 |
| Disgust | 0.13694 |
| Fear | 0.094699 |
| Joy | 0.092905 |
| Sadness | 0.191873 |

**Figure 10.1: Displayr**

Based on this analysis, you can see that for the Entity (Donald Trump), the overall Sentiment is positive, but there is no real emotional significance along the five dimensions. The author is not displaying any of the five emotions (greater than 0.5) in this article. So we can conclude from this analysis that the author is being neutral toward Trump in this article.

Now, let's determine whether this author is an Android or iPhone fan. The results are as follows:

| Entity | Relevance | Sentiment | Type |
|--------|-----------|-----------|------|
| Android | 0.800116 | neutral | OperatingSystem |

| Emotion | Score |
|---------|-------|
| Anger | 0.134284 |
| Disgust | 0.009934 |
| Fear | 0.018486 |
| Joy | 0.682603 |
| Sadness | 0.092229 |

**Figure 10.2: Displayr**

Here we see that for the Entity (Android) the Sentiment is neutral, but we can also see some significance with the emotion Joy. We can conclude that this person seems to like Androids. What about iPhones?

| Entity | Relevance | Sentiment | Type |
|--------|-----------|-----------|------------|
| iPhone | 0.61855 | neutral | Technology |

| Emotion | Score |
|---------|-----------|
| Anger | 0.119744 |
| Disgust | 0.020805 |
| Fear | 0.027743 |
| Joy | 0.559307 |
| Sadness | 0.084753 |

**Figure 10.3: Displayr**

The analysis reveals that under the Entity iPhone, the Sentiment is also neutral but we do see a drop (0.682603 to 0.559307) in the emotion Joy.

**Hypothesis:** This person is politically neutral and uses an Android phone.

Now, it's impossible to draw any conclusion from one article or data set, but we can form an initial hypothesis about this person. From this point on, we'd seek to find more information to confirm whether our hypothesis is true.

Another obvious use of this technology in sales is the analysis of social media traffic for determination of emotions that might be associated with a company's brand. Whether you're posting on LinkedIn, Facebook, Twitter, or blogs, analyses generated by the Emotional Analysis API will allow the company to be mindful of how it's communicating with clients in the marketplace.

For example, when an article is written about your company, you may be unsure as to how some of the comments might be perceived. By simply copying and pasting the article into the analysis, you'll be provided a more objective perspective as to how others are perceiving the article. An example might be a harsh post on Twitter about how your company handled a customer's complaint. Using Sentiment Analysis, you'll be able to identify the post using the keywords or phrases used and use the Emotional Analysis tool to gauge or score the severity of the posting.

Emotional Analysis can also aid in prioritizing response to clients. For example, if after running the analysis you discover that you have several posts that need your attention, you can begin by addressing the Angry ones first, move on to those who may be expressing Disgust, and then finally answer those who are Sad about how your product or service let them down. This is perhaps a new take on "Squeaky wheel gets the grease," but still effective nonetheless.

## Watch Your Tone

Every successful salesperson is aware that any form of customer contact is highly nuanced. Among other things, this implies we must be careful of the "messages" we send in all our communications, and this is yet another area where Emotional Analysis can be employed to advantage.

For example, the Emotional Analysis API might be configured to monitor the "tone" of your own communications, whether it's a social media posting, a proposal being sent to a client, or a response to an email from a client who has a question or concern. The fact is, many sales are lost because of a miscommunication via text or email. The ability to know the tone is correct before you hit that "send" button that can mean the difference between winning and losing a million-dollar deal.

Miscommunication is one of the biggest reasons why deals fall apart. Either we didn't communicate the value of product, or we didn't communicate effectively how our company could serve the client better than the competitor. The toughest thing to communicate to any client is empathy—that we really understand the pressure they might be feeling, the depth of their concerns, or the urgency of a need. Language matters, and how we phrase things signals our level of understanding of the client, their business, and their problems.

As a society, we are moving more toward communicating via text instead of by phone. Studies have shown that executives prefer to be contacted via email, social media channels such as LinkedIn, or text. The more we shift to text, the better we need to become in communicating our expertise and empathy. A new addition to the AlchemyLanguage suite that can help us communicate more effectively via writing of virtually any form is their Tone Analyzer.

Here's a not-so-brief explanation of the science behind the service, and then we'll talk about how we can use it on a daily basis:

The IBM Watson™ Tone Analyzer service is based on the theory of psycholinguistics, a field of research that explores the relationship between linguistic behavior and psychological theories. The service uses linguistic analysis to determine the correlation between the linguistic features of written text and the emotional and language tones to develop scores for each of these tone dimensions.

Psycholinguistics researchers have worked to understand whether the words that we use in our day-to-day lives reflect who we are, how we feel, and how we think. After several decades of research in this area, it is now accepted in psychology, marketing, and other fields that language reflects more than just what we want to say. The frequency with which we use certain types of words can provide clues to personality, thinking style, social connections, and emotional states.

For example, people exhibit various tones in their daily communications: joyful or sad, open or conservative, analytical or informal (Gou et al., 2014, and Jian et al., 2014). These tones can impact the perception of a person's online identity and the effectiveness of their communications in different contexts.

Moreover, in business email communications, people are likely to perceive negative emotions with greater intensity than they do positive emotions (Byron, 2008). And in social media, people present different online identities that impact the impression that others have of them (DiMicco & Millen, 2007).

Many people naturally read a message and judge the tones conveyed by the sender. But can a computer detect the tones disclosed by a message accurately and automatically? This is one of the many challenging questions to which researchers in the artificial intelligence and cognitive sciences fields are seeking answers. First with the Personality Insights service and now with the Tone Analyzer service, IBM is beginning to answer this question.

Research has shown a strong and statistically significant correlation between word choice and personality, emotions, attitudes, intrinsic needs, values, and thought processes. Several researchers have found that people vary in how often they use certain categories of words when writing for blogs, essays, and tweets, and that these communication mediums can help predict different aspects of personality.

Most of these prior works are based on finding psychologically meaningful word categories from word usage in writing. This research serves as the basis for IBM's work on the Tone Analyzer service. Relying on the scientific findings from psycholinguistics research, IBM is working to infer people's personality characteristics, their thinking and writing styles, their emotions, and their intrinsic needs and values from the words that they write. IBM uses its machine-learning models to evaluate these characteristics by assessing various features of a person's writing.[28]

Now, what makes the Tone Analyzer a powerful tool in the IBM Watson language-processing family is the ability to accurately gauge a prospect's interest when responding to a salesperson's email or an email requesting more information. The prospect's tone may correlate to their level of interest and sense of urgency.

For example, I received this email requesting some advice, and I want to determine the likelihood of this potential client buying our sales training program:

---

[28] "The Science Behind the Service." IBM. https://console.bluemix.net/docs/services/tone-analyzer/science.html#the-science-behind-the-service

*Hello Victor,*

*I noticed that you sometimes answer people's questions in your videos and give advice. Thank you for having those videos, I have certainly benefited from them. I have been in B2B sales for several years and my company has a new product that we offer.*
*One of the markets is to automotive repair. The product requires them to charge a few percent more to their customers but it can greatly reduce their expenses at their business. Their biggest concern is if they would lose business to the competition for the few extra percent, although many businesses clearly see the value in what it can do for them.*
*For the ones who have that concern, do you have any suggestions on the best way to handle that? The way I do it now is making them think about how many customers they would actually have to lose over such as a small increase to not make it worth it and talk about how their business is built on repeat and customer loyalty and they won't lose that trust people give them because of something like that. I appreciate you taking the time.*

*Take care,*

Jane Public (real name withheld)

How should I assess Jane's commitment to really solving her problem? Does this email warrant a follow-up call? Salient questions include: How motivated is she? Has she given up on being able to sell into this market? Now, let's assume for a moment that I would like to have Jane sign up for my online sales training program, the Sales Mastery Academy.[29] I get an average of 25 emails, texts, or posts per day from people seeking my help. I can't help everyone, so I have to prioritize who I call back versus who gets a follow-up email only.

IBM uses linguistic analysis to detect joyful, fearful, sad, angry, analytical, confident, and tentative tones that might be found in text. In this case, my goal is to get a better sense of who this individual is and her state of mind, and I'll be using Watson's Tone Analyzer for that purpose. Beyond the text, I want to know more about her personality so that before I pick up the phone and call or respond via email, I'll be better equipped to respond appropriately.

In using IBM's Tone Analyzer,[30] I simply cut and paste the email into the dialogue box, select the type of text being pasted (Email Message), and click Analyze.

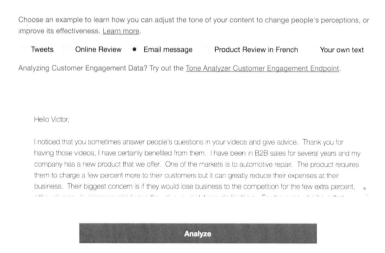

**Figure 11: IBM Watson's Tone Analyzer API**

---

[29] You can find more information at http://www.SalesMasteryAcademy.us

[30] https://www.ibm.com/watson/services/tone-analyzer

Within seconds, the results are presented to me along the five tonal dimensions, described as follows:

**Analytical:** A person's reasoning and analytical attitude about things.

**Confident:** A person's degree of certainty.

**Joy:** Joy or happiness has shades of enjoyment, satisfaction, and pleasure. There is a sense of well-being, inner peace, love, safety, and contentment.

**Sadness:** Indicates a feeling of loss and disadvantage. When a person can be observed to be quiet, less energetic, and withdrawn, it may be inferred that sadness exists.

**Tentative:** A person's degree of inhibition.

The IBM Watson Tone Analyzer allows you to perform text analysis on two different levels, "the document level and the sentence level. Use the document level analysis to get a sense of the overall tone of the document, and use the sentence level analysis to identify specific areas of your content where tones are the strongest."

However, before we get into the results, it's worth pausing for a moment to understand and appreciate how powerful this tool actually is, and how useful it can be in helping salespeople do-what-they-do.

The Tone Analyzer is examining the overall document to get a feel for what the prospect is trying to communicate. But more importantly, the machine can focus in on specific remarks to give the salesperson a clue of the acute pain points of the prospect.

Having such information at hand will then enable the salesperson to *color* subsequent conversation with the prospect.

I use the word "color" intentionally to highlight that our communications are often driven by our state of mind. If we're having a particularly bad day, that mood might color how we interpret a communication or what someone might have said to us. If we're in a foul mood, we may interpret the prospect's request with annoyance and respond accordingly. Or, regardless of mood, we may not be able to grasp the level of concern the prospect is trying to communicate.

Either way, the Tone Analyzer removes any mood bias from the email, providing a more objective interpretation so that we can respond with certainty and clarity. So, let's now look at the results of the email I received from Jane Public by first starting at the document level.

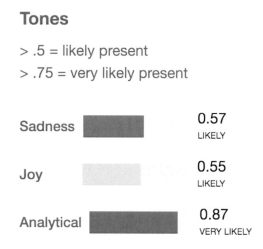

# Document-level

## Tones

> .5 = likely present
> .75 = very likely present

| | | |
|---|---|---|
| Sadness | | 0.57 LIKELY |
| Joy | | 0.55 LIKELY |
| Analytical | | 0.87 VERY LIKELY |

**Figure 12: Tone Analyzer results at the Document Level**

The overall tone of the document is highly analytical (0.87), which tells me that Jane wants a well-thought-out response to her problem. At the emotional level, I'll have to assume she's emotionally neutral (i.e., not sad, not happy). Of course, this isn't a lot to go on from a sales standpoint, so maybe I want to drill down to analyze her sentences and see if I can garner any further insight. The Tone Analyzer can now highlight sentences to indicate the likelihood of a given tone being present. If there is more than one tone present, the Tone Analyzer will show you the differences in strength along that tonal dimension.

**Figure 13: Tone Analysis of the first sentence in the email**

By clicking on the first sentence in the email received, I can see that Jane is highly analytical, and there's also an indication of being tentative. This makes sense since she is building up to asking me for a favor (i.e., help). Since I do not have any history with Jane, some "tentativeness" makes perfect sense.

Now, if I go to the following sentence—"Thank you for having those videos, I have certainly benefited from them"—and click on it, I can see a high degree of confidence and joy in this statement. From a salesperson's standpoint, it's great to see these scores.

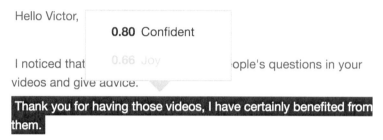

**Figure 13.2: Tone Analyzer detects Joy and Confidence**

Now, let's flip this scenario for a minute to gain an appreciation of the true power of the Tone Analyzer. Let's say that we have to respond via email or text to a proposal that, if you win, is worth a great deal of business.

Your goal is to construct an email that sounds confident, transmits to the client that you are excited to work with him (joy), and you also want to demonstrate your analytical skills in how you will approach his problem and help him develop a solution. The Tone Analyzer will allow you to craft a response that ranks high on the crucial emotional tones: Analytic, Confident, and Joy.

Today we send out emails, texts, or documents with minor consideration to the sentiment, emotion, or tone contained therein. In future, the machines we've been speaking of will be able to construct the appropriate level of response on your behalf with the appropriate tones.

As the machine learns from the number of sales deals won and lost, it will be able to analyze all emails, texts, documents, and proposals associated with deals that were won and of course incrementally learn from all such data in creating an even stronger algorithm with each new data event. Stated differently, every time a deal is won or lost, that information is fed into the machine so that it can learn which communications are most effective. This is a powerful idea.

Humans are social creatures, and social creatures communicate. The implication here is that anything that impacts communication (e.g., intent, tone, emotion) affects the humans involved, and this is something the salesperson can leverage to mutual advantage.

It's estimated that salespeople spend about 20–40% of their time on tasks that are not associated with client interaction. If using supervised Machine Learning to draft responses, small proposals, budgetary estimates, responses to Requests for Proposals (RFPs), or Requests for Information (RFIs), the salesperson can in principle reduce their administrative burden by 10–20%, the implied cost savings of which would be considerable. If these documents could also include Sentiment, Emotional, and Tone Analysis and increase the salesperson's close rate by 5%-10%--and this is a conservative estimate—imagine what effect that might have on a company's top-line revenue.

The bottom line here is that any ability to use Machine Learning as a means to lower administrative burden (i.e., time, effort, and cost) and increase close rate will help companies become more profitable. And it goes without saying that the salesforce would be happier and more productive. This, in turn, reduces churn rates, associated hiring costs, and what have you.

Takeaways:

- How we communicate is critically important in winning more business or connecting with clients.

- Using Sentiment and Emotional Analysis tools will give salespeople the power to construct better email communications and customer proposals.

- Using Machine Learning to monitor social media channels for any comments regarding our company will (a) alert the company that a comment has been made and (b) allow a company to respond appropriately.

# CHAPTER 8

# Amazon's Renaissance

The road to utilization, commercialization, and arguably commoditization of artificial intelligence must certainly pass by Seattle, Washington, the home of Amazon, Inc. What started as an innocuous online bookstore has transformed itself into the largest Internet-based retailer in the world as measured by total sales and market capitalization.

Founded in 1994 by Jeff Bezos, Amazon has become a serial disruptor in many industries from movies to music to retail. Amazon's ability to stock a variety of products, distribute through various channels, and deliver "anywhere and anytime" has wreaked havoc on many brick-and-mortar stores throughout the United States.

Amazon has also moved to the front of the pack in technology, supply chain management, logistics, and now, artificial intelligence deployment in service of the consumer market. Whether it was planned out with much foresight or by virtue of a gradual realization, Amazon's view of the future isn't driven by market trends, but by the aggregation of data. And when I say data, I don't mean just Big Data; I mean *huge* data.

Data is the new "oil," and Amazon is scouring the market to find rich fields in the form of data repositories and develop new means of drilling for more "juice" in the form of human data. The former is all about purchases and acquiring while the latter is about infiltrating our homes and personal lives to gather more intelligence on our daily habits. Why? Because Amazon has realized this is a direct line to more profit.

Many companies now employ strategies to collect data as more and more are realizing that customer data is an asset with a tangible value. Those 1s and 0s have more than just Boolean value; they have financial value for any company that can aggregate, analyze, and take action with the information that can be extracted from customer data.

Far from the First Industrial Revolution's model of assets being a physical thing you might find at a factory or office, today's assets are stored on hard drives somewhere in the cloud. Companies today are either mining their data for information or acquiring new data sets (i.e., buying sources of data) with the hope of using advanced analytics engines to reveal some new market strategy or new product to be developed, or to create a new revenue stream. Continuing the analogy, Amazon is sitting on top of one of the largest data repositories worldwide, and they have every intention of mining the hell out of it. We're not just taking data—we're talking data specific to patterns of human consumption.

The amount and diversity of products bought each day from the Amazon site are staggering, and there seems to be no apparent end in sight to Amazon's ability to satisfy a consumer's whimsical need or want. *Business Insider*'s Jay Yarow listed some fun facts on how much customers are buying from the Amazon site:

- Customers ordered more than 26.5 million items worldwide across all product categories, which is a record-breaking 306 items per second.

- Amazon customers purchased more than one toy per second on mobile devices.

- Amazon customers purchased enough copies of the "Fifty Shades" trilogy by E.L. James, including *Fifty Shades of Grey, Fifty Shades Darker, Fifty Shades Freed*, and the trilogy box set, to create a stack 445 times taller than the Space Needle.

- The cumulative weight of the "Bond 50" Blu-ray sets purchased by Amazon customers this holiday season would be 800 times the weight of Daniel Craig.

- Amazon customers purchased enough TVs to cover the field of every NFL stadium.

- Amazon customers purchased enough vinyl copies of The Beatles albums that if laid flat would extend 20 times the length of Abbey Road in London.

- The Amazon MP3 store has sold enough music for everyone at Woodstock '69 to jam out to another three days of music for peace and love.

- If you stacked every Christmas Story Leg Lamp purchased by Amazon customers this holiday season, the height would reach the top of Mt. Everest.

- Amazon customers purchased enough Angry Birds plush toys to stretch 285 times the height of the tallest tree in the world, located in California's Redwood Forest.

- Amazon's third-party sellers sold enough Lindt truffles to serve one to every traveler passing through Chicago's O'Hare Airport over a weekend.

- Amazon's third-party sellers sold enough HDMI cables to make three round-trips to the International Space Station.

- Amazon customers added more than 15 million toys to their Wish Lists this holiday season.

And my personal favorite:

- Amazon customers purchased enough sports team garden gnomes to fill every seat in Madison Square Garden.[31]

The real value in this seeming polyglot of facts isn't just in the revenues generated from these purchases, but also in the amount of telling data that can be extracted from such a diverse constellation of idiosyncrasies exhibited on the part of these consumers.

The machine algorithms must be feasting on this rich harvest of diverse data sets while data scientists rub their hands together in anticipation of what actionable insights their predictive analytics will produce.

---

[31] Yarow, Jay. "Amazon Was Selling 306 Items Every Second At Its Peak This Year." *Business Insider,* December 2012.
http://www.businessinsider.com/amazon-holiday-facts-2012-12

The resulting challenge for Amazon is to somehow leverage the data it collects to better serve today's "I want it now" customer base. If artificial intelligence has a virtuous circle, this is it; the more data the machine collects, the smarter it gets, the more it can anticipate your needs, the more you will buy, which of course results in more data for the machine to collect. It's what you might call a "Win-Win" scenario!

## Alexa, The Trojan Horse

In 1877, Thomas Edison invented the first phonograph that could mechanically record sound, using a rotating cylinder wrapped in a tinfoil sheet. Sound vibrations would trigger a stylus, which impressed the tinfoil with grooves corresponding to the pitch. This cylinder could then be played back to recreate the speech or music that had been engraved onto it.[32]

Note that the phonograph could only play what was recorded onto its rotating cylinder. Fast-forward to the present, and we now have a similar-looking cylinder that can record what you say and play back what is spoken. But that's where the similarities between Edison's cylinder and Amazon's cylinder end.

Alexa is a personal assistant developed by Amazon to make your life just a little bit easier. Need to know the weather? Just ask Alexa. Need directions to the mall? Ask Alexa. What to know how the stock market is doing? Ask Alexa. In the mood to hear your favorite song,? Just ask Alexa.

Developed and sold by Amazon, Alexa is capable of voice interaction, music playback, making to-do lists, setting alarms, streaming podcasts, playing audiobooks, and providing weather, traffic, and other real-time information, such as news. Alexa can

---

[32] "Phonograph." Wikipedia. https://en.wikipedia.org/wiki/Phonograph

also control several smart devices (e.g., your thermostat, in-home camera, smoke detector, TV, and so forth). In effect, Alexa becomes a home automation system.

With all these features and functionalities, you would think that this device would cost you at least a few month's pay. Not so! For the equivalent of few day's pay, earning minimum wage at that, you can own this powerful technology. Amazon has made this device affordable to the masses.

One might argue that the reason the price is so low is due to the volume of devices being sold, driving down the manufacturing cost (i.e., supply and demand).

The other reason might be that Amazon isn't really concerned about making a profit on the device, but is more concerned about getting you to bring the device into your home. For what purpose, you might ask? Well, the purpose of this seeming generosity is to collect data on you! Why? So they can market to you more effectively.

Marketing has always been responsive to what consumers do, say, or buy, and a game of guessing what consumers might want. Marketing's access to your innermost desires ends at the front door to your apartment or home.

We Americans are very protective of our privacy. The less people know about us, the safer we feel from con-men or charlatans. It's human nature not to divulge too much information for fear of it being used against you or worse, to harm you. Yet something fascinating is happening, and the American consumer is complicit in its execution. American privacy is being invaded by outside companies with little or no resistance by consumers.

The Trojan horse tale originates, of course, from the Trojan War. After a decade-long stalemate in their war against Troy, the Greeks finally decide to switch tactics. They construct a massive wooden horse and leave it before the city gates, and the Greek fleet briefly departs from the shore. A false Greek deserter then informs the Trojans that the horse is an offering to Athena, and that by taking the horse into the city, the Trojans will win the goddess's favor instead of the Greeks. Ignoring the desperate warnings of Cassandra, the Trojans do as the "deserter" suggests, unaware that a force of Greek soldiers is concealed with the horse. This force emerges at night and opens the city gates, and the returning Greek army rushes in to sack the city.

Any scheme by an enemy to gain an invitation to within a target's "walls" can thus be called a Trojan horse. The most famous modern examples are "Trojan horse" viruses, or simply "Trojans," which deceive users themselves into installing malicious code.[33]

Could Alexa then be considered a Trojan horse (sans the maliciousness and trickery)? By activating Alexa in your home and setting it to listening mode, are we not inviting an outside source (Amazon) to "listen and gather" information on our daily habits and desires? Many people who've purchased Alexa view it as a personal assistant that will make their life just a bit easier or at a minimum, a bit more convenient.

The question of import is, "Is Amazon listening?" I'd guess the answer is "no," at least in the audible human sense. I don't believe that Amazon is listening to our conversations, but I'm quite sure the machines are listening on some level. The machines are listening to our requests, using Natural Language Processing, which are algorithms designed to transcribe and parse our words, creating unstructured data that will be used by the machine. For what purpose? I'm sure if you ask Jeff Bezos, he

---

[33] "Trojan Horse." Wikipedia.
https://en.wikipedia.org/wiki/Trojan_Horse

would assert that by virtue of knowing and anticipating your needs and wants, Amazon is that much better able to serve you.

However, this altruistic notion is also tied to a profit motive. The more the company knows about you, the more they can find ways to serve you better, and in true quid pro quo fashion serve themselves as well through the increased revenues and shareholder value thus obtained.

Alexa is a cloud-based voice service acting as a personal assistant, but it is also a data collection device. In particular, Alexa can communicate (i.e., exchange information) with third-party devices developed by other manufacturers. In other words, Alexa can also be a gateway for other companies to collect data on your behaviors.

For example, Apple's Nest thermostat monitors your in-home environment. Nest knows several things about your habits: it knows when you are home or away, it knows (on average) how much time you spend in your house, and it learns to predict your presence in the home from day-to-day. Alexa can communicate with Nest to collect more data on your in-home behavior. If you decide to order a movie or pizza or send a message to a friend, Alexa is listening and learning from you, and so are the devices connected to it.

Alexa uses Natural Language Understanding and Automated Speech Recognition with Deep Learning to understand and execute your commands. As a Deep Learning construct, the algorithm learns and understands the more you speak to it. When Alexa gets your request wrong, the Deep Learning algorithm is already learning how to avoid making that mistake in the future. Alexa is getting smarter and becomes better at understanding your requests in order to serve you better.

## What is Cloud Computing?

Cloud computing is the on-demand delivery of computer power, database storage, applications, and other IT resources through a cloud services platform via the Internet with pay-as-you-go pricing.

## Cloud Computing Basics

Whether you are running applications that share photos to millions of mobile users or you're supporting the critical operations of your business, a cloud services platform provides rapid access to flexible and low cost IT resources. With cloud computing, you don't need to make large upfront investments in hardware and spend a lot of time on the heavy lifting of managing that hardware. Instead, you can provision exactly the right type and size of computing resources you need so as to power your newest bright idea or operate your IT department. You can access as many resources as you need, almost instantly, and only pay for what you use.

## How Does Cloud Computing Work?

Cloud computing provides a simple way to access servers, storage, databases and a broad set of application services over the Internet. A Cloud services platform such as Amazon Web Services owns and maintains the network-connected hardware required for these application services, while you provision and use what you need via a web application.

## Six Advantages and Benefits of Cloud Computing

1) Trade capital expense for variable expense

Instead of having to invest heavily in data centers and servers before you know how you're going to use them, with Cloud you only pay when you consume computing resources, and then only pay for how much you consume.

2) Benefits of the cloud from massive economy of scale

By using cloud computing, you can achieve a lower variable cost than you might get on your own. Because usage from hundreds of thousands of customers are aggregated in the cloud, providers such as Amazon Web Services can achieve higher economies of scale which translates into lower pay-as-you-go prices.

3) Eliminate capacity guesswork

Prior to cloud computing becoming commonplace managers were often compelled to guess at infrastructure capacity needs. The obvious downside to this is when you make a capacity decision prior to actually deploying an application, you more often than not end up sitting on expensive idle resources or dealing with limited capacity. With cloud computing, these problems go away. You can access as much or as little as you need, and scale up and down as required with only a few minutes notice.

4) Increase speed and agility

In a cloud computing environment, new IT resources are effectively "a click away," which means you reduce the time it takes to make those resources available to your developers from weeks to just minutes. This results in a dramatic increase in agility for the organization, since the cost and time it takes to experiment and develop is significantly lower.

5) Stop spending money on running and maintaining data centers
Focus on projects that differentiate your business, not the infrastructure. Cloud computing lets you focus on your own customers, rather than on the heavy lifting of racking, stacking, and powering servers.

6) Go global in minutes
Easily deploy your application in multiple regions around the world with just a few clicks. This means you can provide a lower latency and better experience for your customers simply and at minimal cost.

Source: https://aws.amazon.com/what-is-cloud-computing/

## The Benevolent Giant

Alexa uses both Speech Recognition (SR) and Natural Language Processing (NLP) algorithms to teach itself to understand human language, tone, and equally important, context. The ability to also understand variations in speech patterns (e.g., accents) and sentiment allows Alexa to interact and respond appropriately when a request is made.

The power and application of SR and NLP are growing and being applied in all aspects of customer service or any area where routine tasks or requests can be handled by the machine. The more AI is used in our daily lives, the more power is required to run the machines in terms of computing power and cost. Implementing an AI strategy is not cheap, and it's not like flicking on a light switch to get started—or is it?

A growing number of companies have been looking to jump into the AI fray in order to find ways to grow their revenue stream. Companies want to be able to process data and feed it into a predictive algorithm that delivers actionable insights that will power a marketing strategy into new products, services, or markets. These companies know full well that if they aren't harnessing the power and intelligence of Machine Learning, they are falling behind. Every day that they fail to monetize the data in their databases represents revenues not being captured. For many companies, this could be the difference between hitting their quarterly revenue number or going under.

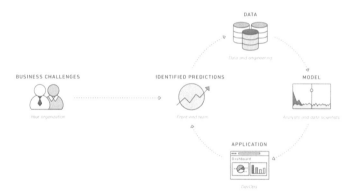

**Figure 14: Amazon's Artificial Intelligence Model**

The sense of urgency to use AI is there, but companies who don't have the market capitalization of Amazon or its revenue streams struggle to implement an AI strategy because of the following:

- The upfront investment in R&D to develop Deep Learning algorithms

- Finding and hiring the right data scientists

- The cost of building and running a data center

- The time involved from getting started to being able to implement and leverage AI in their business and thus see a return on investment

Recognizing the need of many companies and seeing an opportunity to monetize its expertise in cloud-based computing, Amazon in 1996 launched their Amazon Web Services (AWS) product. "Amazon.com started AWS to allow other businesses to enjoy the same IT infrastructure, with agility and cost benefits, and now continues to democratize Machine Learning (ML) technologies to the hands of every business."[34]

Companies can now, for a fee, begin to implement AI into their various processes at a fraction of the cost if they were to attempt to develop the technology themselves.

**Parting the Amazon Cloud**

There are a number of significant advantages in connection with Cloud Computing technology, but how does this factor in with regard to AI and Big Data? A significant clue to a possible answer is found in consideration of deployment trends for analytics software applications of the sort we've been discussing. Increasingly, the generic components—such as image recognition, informatics, data fusion, and data visualization—are being hosted on Internet web servers. The rationale is twofold: (1) increased performance against what are often massive data footprints and (2) amortization of cost over all users.

---

[34] https://aws.amazon.com/amazon-ai/what-is-ai/

Now, when one considers the potential number of users of such services, the cost/benefit trade-off becomes compelling. We've already touched on analytics-based performance enhancement in our previous discussion of AI and Big Data. Here, we look at the cost advantages of using cloud-based applications that might be offered by some provider. In principle, this represents a high-performance entry option to the Big Data world, and at relatively low cost.

Where one considers cloud-based services, two considerations immediately come to mind: (1) ease of deployment and (2) security. In our globalized economy, many companies have distributed business units worldwide. A company may have a corporate headquarters in one country, technology development in another country, manufacturing in yet another country, and marketing/sales distribution functions in still another. The dependence of cloud computing on broadband Internet is consistent with a globally distributed enterprise. In particular, any analytics applications that a given company might develop are easily distributed to any desired business units as a matter of course. This capability is a fundamental component of the entire rationale for cloud computing technology.

Because cloud resources are generally located "elsewhere" and under "other" management control, security is an obvious concern. However, corporate cloud resources are virtual in the sense that any applications development is self-contained within a heavily encrypted environment unavailable to all outsiders. In particular, all data and applications held under the aegis of a given client are secured within this encrypted environment. In practice, security is a non-problem; the fact that cloud technology is at all viable within the enterprise computing market sector is a testimony to the success of this cloud security. In the present context, users of cloud technology need not be concerned that proprietary analytics will be exposed to outside competing interests.

However, with the increasing commoditization of analytics resources, one might envision a circumstance in which many companies are using the same tools to generate their analytics. Thus, it all comes down to "what questions are being asked" or "what analytics are being generated."

One might even anticipate as time wears on that any competitive advantage may be lost among users of such technologies. In essence, the playing field is thus leveled. Of course, there is no limitation on the development of even more sophisticated tools, extending the capability of those generic tools but still remaining unavailable to other cloud users.

We simply point out "AI" and "Big Data" are young technologies, and one must keep pace with new developments in order to compete. Indeed, as always, victory goes to that company that is most clever, asks the right questions, correctly assesses risk, and then acts decisively. Standing back from it all, we see again that these technologies don't replace the human agent but merely multiply a fundamental (human) capability.

**Beneath the Surface**

As Amazon's ecosystem gets more sophisticated and its footprint (data centers) expands, companies using AWS will be able to leverage the intelligence and power found within.

Amazon Lex is a great example of how companies are accelerating their entrance and commitment to using AI so as to streamline their internal processes. Amazon Lex is a service that allows companies to develop conversation chatbots in order to improve the customer experience, minimize mundane tasks, and reduce overall costs. Using Amazon Lex's Deep Learning algorithm, companies can now develop their own chatbots that can grow and learn with every customer conversation. With this new capability to simulate sophisticated natural language content, conversational bots have been democratized to a large extent.

The ability to access and use Amazon's intellectual property (i.e., algorithms) and assets (i.e., datacenters) raises several intriguing questions:

- Why would Amazon do this?

- Why share any of their intellectual property or assets with companies that might try to compete with it?

- With such a large datacenter footprint and corresponding processing power, why not retain that advantage in a market that is so data-driven?

The answer is found in the recurring revenue obtained via through monthly or annual subscriptions. Like any business seeking to create value for its shareholders, Amazon sees the obvious strategic benefit of monetizing its assets (IP and Datacenter) and creating a large and continuous revenue stream.

Thus far, AWS revenues have grown to over $4 billion. I suspect that as AWS continues to grow in terms of revenue and users, the platforms themselves will also evolve. AWS will surely reinvest their profits into building more powerful network platforms armed with an increasing sophistication in their logistics, service management, and Deep Learning applications, such as delivery drones and driverless cars and trucks. In Jeff Bezos' words:

I would say, a lot of the value that we're getting from Machine Learning is actually happening kind of *beneath the surface* [emphasis added]. It is things like improved search results, improved product recommendations for customers, improved forecasting for inventory management, and literally hundreds of other things beneath the surface. We are now solving problems with Machine Learning and artificial intelligence that were in the realm of science fiction for the last several decades. And natural language understanding, machine vision problems, it really is an amazing renaissance... There's no institution in the world that can't be improved by Machine Learning.

When it comes to data collection and how that data is used, we should all be somewhat leery of what lies "beneath the surface." Let us hope that the giant remains benevolent in serving the public good, and its customer base, of course.

Takeaways:

- Data is the new "oil," and Amazon is scouring the market to find rich fields in the form of data repositories and develop new means of drilling for more "juice" in the form of human data.

- Cloud computing is the on-demand delivery of computer power, database storage, applications, and other IT resources through a cloud services platform via the Internet with pay-as-you-go pricing.

- Leveraging already-developed applications will allow companies to move faster in the direction of AI.

CHAPTER **9**

# EI – Email Intelligence

*We are reaching a point where human intervention into the mundane tasks of moving a client along in the sales funnel can be handed over to a cognitive assistant, thereby freeing the salesperson up to focus on those sales-centric activities only a human can do.*

All across America, you take part in a morning ritual along with millions of other Americans. You walk into your office or cubicle, and the first thing you do is fire up the computer. After a minute or so, you click to launch your email browser, and it comes as no surprise that you have over 75 new emails since the night before.

Your first step is a first pass where you delete those that look spammy or otherwise questionable. You delete about 25 and feel a sense of accomplishment as your list has now dwindled to 50. You then proceed to a second pass where you open those emails from your superiors, colleagues, or business relationships.

As you go through these emails, you find some you can quickly answer right away but others require more of your time, so you close them out for later; you "star" or otherwise highlight them to remind you that a response is required and is also time sensitive. You're now down to about 20 emails. This last batch is from people you don't know, so you proceed to open them according to how interesting the headline sounds. Some you save for further reading later, and others you delete until you're down to zero new emails. Does this sound familiar?

A Carleton University study surveyed 1,500 people across six organizations and found some interesting data points regarding emails:

> half reported high levels of work overload and stress, much of it associated with spending so much time—a full one-third of their time at the office—reading and answering emails. They also spend half of the time they work at home on email. And 30 percent of the time, the emails they're getting are neither urgent nor important.

The authors, Linda Duxbury and Andre Lanctot, further commented,

> The results suggest that organizations need to determine how to best help employees cope with widespread email overload and reduce volume through the use of appropriate policies, training, and enforcement... That's 11.7 hours spent at work and 5.3 hours at home—every week.[35]

---

[35] "Carleton Study Finds People Spending a Third of Job Time on Email." *Carleton Newsroom.* April 20, 2017.
http://newsroom.carleton.ca/2017/04/20/carleton-study-finds-people-spending-third-job-time-email/

Here are the key insights from the study:

- Employees are spending 33% of their time on email in the workplace.

- When they work from home, they spend 50% reading and answering emails.

- Each week, the "typical" knowledge worker spends 11.7 processing email at work and 5.3 hours from home, for a total of 17 hours or a third of their work week.

- Each day, they send/receive 86 work-related emails at work and 25 from home.

- Those who participated in the survey reported missing three days of work in a six-month period due to emotional fatigue.

- One in five reported thinking weekly about leaving their jobs.

The study goes on to provide some recommendations for how a company can decrease the load to improve the employees' well-being.

- Reduce the employee's expectations of how quickly they have to respond to an email. (My response: But what if the items are critical and they have to be done by a specific time?)

- Hire a "floater" to handle straightforward email at peak periods. (My response: What if that isn't economically feasible or impossible? What if it does require a trained employee to filter what's important and what's not important?)

- Invest in better spam blockers. (My response: Most companies have some type of spam blocker installed, but it's not 100% guaranteed. This is a cat and mouse game. When you install a better blocker, the spammers develop a way to get around it.)

- Develop workplace policy that spells out who should send what to whom and when. (My response: Not very realistic when you have many employees. Imagine having to "review" a list before you send things out. What happens when you do have to send something to someone not on your list?)

- Encourage personal strategies to manage email; pick a specific time to respond each day. (My response: This is a great idea until you have to deal with many time-sensitive issues.)

- Offer training about tools to manage email. (My response: This is the perfect segue into how AI can help.)

Another study released by The Radicati Group (TRG), a technology market research firm, looked at email exchanges within workplaces on a global scale. Some of their findings are both fascinating and disturbing. TRG estimates that the number of business and consumer emails that will be sent and received per day in 2017 will be around 269 billion. That number will climb to about 320 billion by 2021. They also say the average office worker receives 121 emails daily, almost 50 percent of which is spam.[36]

The problem of emails will continue to be more of an issue moving forward. Before jumping into how artificial intelligence can help us with handling emails effectively, we need to address some other issues to fully understand how an inefficient email strategy hurts business.

For example, the Carleton University study only speaks to the number of hours spent on emails and the lost hours of productivity. What it doesn't address is how many opportunities are missed because, in this case, the salesperson was overwhelmed by email inquiries and requests. How many deals are lost because the salesperson never responded to prospects' requests/inquiries? How many deals are lost because the salesperson, being overwhelmed by emails, rushed through a response and didn't answer the prospect's question completely?

The true cost of an ineffective email strategy or tools can only be calculated by estimating the lost hours of productivity (e.g., 11.7 hours x # of Employees) and quantifying the revenue lost (e.g., # of Deals x Average Order Size) from missed opportunities.

## Artificial (Email) Intelligence

Google has now stepped into the email management void, using machine language to assist Gmail users respond to inquiries with a simple click of a button. If you're a Gmail user, you're familiar with the new auto-responder feature. When an email is sent to

---

[36] *Email Statistics Report, 2017–2021.* The Radicati Group, 2017. http://www.radicati.com/wp/wp-content/uploads/2017/01/Email-Statistics-Report-2017-2021-Executive-Summary.pdf

you, you are given three response options to choose from. For example, this morning I received an email with the subject line: Important. When I opened the email, there was no text in the body but instead just a graphic I had requested attached. Upon opening the email from my mobile device, Google gave me three response options:

- Got it, thanks!
- Got it!
- Received, thank you.

I then opened a second email from a colleague of mine who just sent over a long list of suggestions on a project we're working on. Google gave the following response button suggestions:

- Sounds good!
- Sounds like a plan!
- Sounds good, thanks!

Google is using Machine Learning along with Natural Language Processing to first mine the information in the subject line, text in the email, and then attachments so it can form an appropriate response. Notice that in the first email where only the subject line contained data ("Important") with no text in the email, Google's response options were more restrained (Got it!) when compared to the second email (Sounds like a plan!).

The algorithm used by Google also performs Sentiment Analysis, which can detect or sense the emotional disposition of a sender and respond accordingly. Now, while these responses may seem rudimentary for now, one can only imagine what the future might hold. As you respond to more of the emails sent to you, the machine will begin to learn more about your customers or colleagues, and more importantly, it will learn more about you.

Can you imagine a future where the machine will be able to respond for you better than you might have responded yourself? Can you imagine a time when you'll no longer have to sift through your emails? The machine will sift through the emails for you, gauge their urgency, prioritize them, and respond to time-sensitive emails for you.

Although artificial intelligence is still a bit away from that Utopian dream of completely autonomous AI Auto-responders, there are companies making small but significant strides in that direction. A good example is a company called Boomerang, which offers an AI plug-in to Gmail (and Outlook) called "Respondable" that can help sift, store, auto-recall, and prioritize your emails more "intelligently."

One cool feature allows you to hit the "snooze button" on certain messages, which means they will disappear from your email list and reappear in a preset period of time. Just like when you hit your snooze button and it will remind you in 10 minutes to wake up, Respondable will remind you to look at a previously "snoozed" email.

Respondable can also analyze your messages as you write them and, even more impressive, apply predictive analytics based on historical emails to predict how likely you are to get a response from the sender. The plug-in can even provide some suggestions on how you might improve your email so as to render a response more likely. Suggestions are generated along these dimensions:

- Subject Length
- Word Count
- Questions Count
- Reading Level

- Advanced Features
- Positivity
- Politeness
- Subjectivity

As you write the body of your email, Respondable shows you whether you're likely to get a response. For example, writing this email to your customer will not, according to Respondable, result in a response.

> I'm following up from our meeting on Wednesday and to explore opportunities to strengthen our engagement. Let me know if we can discuss.

**Figure 15: Respondable's User Interface**

However, by simply adding an "invite," the chances of getting a positive response are dramatically improved.

> I'm following up from our meeting on Wednesday and to explore opportunities to strengthen our engagement. Let me know if we can discuss. **Are you free for coffee on Friday**?

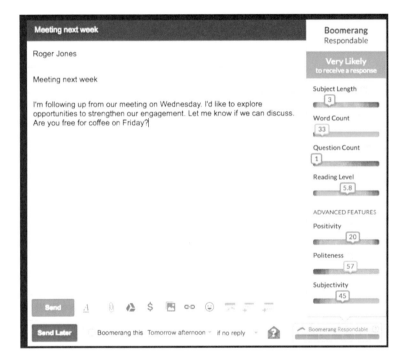

**Figure 16: Respondable's User Interface**

This application will modify the ratings on the right-hand side as you type your subject line or the actual message. For example, if your subject line isn't compelling enough, you may get a 1 or 2 for Subject Length. If the subject line is too direct and may need some softening, the application will let you know. As you modify, you can dynamically see the scores along the bars change.

Having this AI assistant at your disposal will definitely assist in crafting a better subject line and a better email. And again, with every email interaction, the machine updates its algorithm to reflect what subject lines or body text will resonate better with your intended target client.

The goal is to get the prospect or client to respond to a specific request. Whether you're asking for a meeting or feedback on a field demonstration, the ability to use AI to craft a response-worthy email gives the salesperson an edge over his competitors. This is a prime example of AI augmenting a salesperson's ability to close more deals through Machine Learning.

*Wired* magazine recently wrote of Boomerang:

> Boomerang is in a unique position to offer this particular service. In addition to helping you snooze emails, the plugin can also remind you about emails you're waiting on a response to. That gives the company a nice big set of data about which emails receive responses and which don't. While companies like Google and Microsoft obviously have access to much bigger piles of email, Boomerang CEO Alex Moore says his company's approach may be more accurate. "Gmail is going to see a lot of email that people aren't necessarily expecting a reply to," he explains. But users are clearly expecting to receive responses to the messages they ask Boomerang to monitor. The algorithms are a mix of different AI approaches, including Deep Learning, a branch of AI benefitting from a wealth of research and open source software released by big name companies, including Google, Facebook, and Microsoft. Moore says the most surprising thing the team learned is that responses drop-off significantly for emails that use language above about

a sixth grade reading level, but emails that are too simple tend to be ignored as well. A 3rd grade reading level is optimal. He was also surprised that neutral emails tend to receive fewer responses than positive or negative emails. In short, being too negative is bad, but being slightly negative is better than being boring.[37]

Let's get back to time management. How much more effective will salespeople be when they can use an application that can tell them the strength of their subject line and actual email text? How will this increase their response rate, and what will that mean in terms of closing more deals? The probability of closing a sale increases dramatically when a salesperson is able to (a) reach the decision maker and (b) be able to set up a meeting. Thus, with an improved success rate for these tasks, applications like Respondable will also improve the close rate. And as these AI applications get smarter with every email iteration, so too will the ability to craft compelling emails that generate results.

Respondable's "snooze button" is also a simple but effective time management tool. Emails that used to get lost in the mix are less likely to be missed or forgotten, and the client is that much more likely to receive a timely response, which of course further increases the chances of closing a sale. One can only imagine how this simple feature will help companies capture revenue that would have otherwise been lost to human error or inattentiveness.

I envision that as the machine learns more through email interactions, that there will come a time when the machine is able to draw a correlation between the time it takes to respond to an

---

[37] Finley, Klint. "AI is Here to Help You Write Emails People Will Actually Read." *Wired*, August 2016. https://www.wired.com/2016/08/boomerang-using-ai-help-send-better-email/

email and a sales close rate. I suspect the machine will confirm what we all know intuitively: the faster a salesperson responds to a potential client with a well-crafted email, the more likely she is to close the deal. Moreover, the machine will also be able to find the hidden patterns we aren't able to see. For example, which emails need to be treated as high priority vs. low? What is the best time to respond? What must the content include? How long should the email be? In terms of tone, what word or word combinations should be used to transmit the right sentiment? What time of day should we send it?

In the not-too-distant future, the machine will respond on our behalf based on sentiment, content, and timing. Yes, the machine will be able to prioritize our emails, construct the content in the email, and determine the tone and even the best time to send it. A company called Phrasee is already moving strongly in that direction.

Phrasee is a language optimization application that, according to the company, "gives you human-sounding, machine-optimized email marketing language that gets you more opens, clicks, and conversions."[38] Phrasee's artificial intelligence algorithms use a language analysis tool that will aid in the creation of your subject line, body copy, and a call-to-action. Its algorithm will datamine hundreds of emotions, sentiments, and phrases, and then predict what your target client (prospect) is most likely to respond to.

Like all good Machine Learning algorithms, the more you use it, the more results it receives, which of course means the "smarter" it will get over time. The future of emailing will forever be changed when machines will be able to take over the majority of email tasks for the salesperson. Will they do everything, making

---

[38] "How It Works." Phrasee. https://phrasee.co/how-it-works/

our email interactions obsolete? I don't think so. At the end of the day, we're dealing with humans who will need a human touch.

As previously observed, salespeople today spend anywhere from 30% to 50% on activities that have nothing to do with the actual act of selling (i.e., answering emails, meeting with clients, calling them up, doing demos, etc.). If AI apps like Respondable or Phrasee can knock that number down by 20 or 30%, total sales and the company's revenue will be significantly impacted. Machine Learning applications like Respondable and Phrasee will augment our ability to serve more clients better. The mundane, time-consuming, but still necessary task of managing email communications will largely be relegated to the machine. The upshot is that the derived benefit of just this AI tool alone is huge!

The ability of Machine Learning to absorb some of the salesperson's rudimentary or remedial tasks was not so very long ago thought of as science fiction, something out there in the future. However, when it comes to Artificial Email Intelligence, the future is right around the corner.

More companies will be jumping into this space soon enough, and I predict that email marketing, not just sales, will go through an AI transformation. These applications can also be used to construct newsletters, press releases, annual reports, and so on. The future of Language Processing, Predictive Analysis, and Sentiment Analysis are already converging. Just consider that as you scroll through your emails, you've probably read some written by a machine.

Key Takeaways

- The average employee spends 11.7 hours on emails at work and 5.3 hours at home—every week.

- Salespeople need help in managing email, responding to emails, and constructing compelling messages.

- Currently there are AI applications that you can use to manage your emails and help you respond appropriately.

- The more you use a Machine Learning-based email assistant, the smarter it gets.

- In the future, you won't have to manage or respond to the majority of your emails; the machine will handle that for you.

CHAPTER **10**

# Hire Smarter

*When a position opens up, so too does the floodgate for resumes. Normally, screening, hiring, and retention are cumbersome and ineffective processes that don't always yield the best hire. With predictive analytics in artificial intelligence, numerous relevant variables are carefully considered and weighed in less than a couple of hours or even minutes.*

In an organized hiring and screening process, the natural first step is to determine which traits your salespeople need in order to succeed and the relative importance of those traits. These traits are chosen because they are thought to be predictors of success, whether it is based on prevailing wisdom (smarter candidates will perform better) or anecdotal evidence from past experience. A manager would use a scorecard to outline what she's looking for. It might look something like this:

| Traits | Candidate #1 Rank (1–10) | Candidate #2 Rank (1–10) |
|---|---|---|
| Intelligence | 4 | 6 |
| Coachable | 5 | 2 |
| Closing Skills | 3 | 5 |
| Team Player | 7 | 3 |
| Score: | 27 | 24 |

Preference is given to those candidates who can score the highest on all of the areas each manager deems to be important predictors of success.

Though managers are aiming for objectivity here, how can we be sure that those traits are actually going to lead to better hires or if the method of evaluation is actually valid? Even with the most experienced of hiring managers, certainty is not guaranteed.

Daniel Kahneman, author of *Thinking, Fast and Slow*, tried to create a better evaluation system for new recruits in the Israeli Army. He found that even the most experienced senior officers' predictions had no correlation with successful recruits. It was clear that a "gut feeling" was not a reliable decision-making tool.

Where there is human prediction, there is also subjectivity and plenty of room for biases. Human biases are an evolutionary result of an overstimulated brain; you use shortcuts and generalizations to save processing energy in your decision-making and critical thinking apparatus. Although this approach to things suited the first *Homo sapiens*, it's not beneficial for today's talent acquisition processes. Some of the more prevalent shortcuts we use to predict who will be a productive employee are:

1. Availability Heuristic: Wikipedia defines this as the tendency to overestimate the likelihood of events, which

can be influenced by how recent, unusual or emotionally charged they may be.[39] For example, if someone you admired went to a specific school, wouldn't you be more likely to hold that school, even without any knowledge of their academic rigor, in high esteem?

2. Confirmation Bias: The tendency to search for, interpret, focus on, and remember information in a way that confirms one's preconceptions. Maybe you've been told that intelligence is a great predictor of success, and several of your best salespeople have very high IQs. However, you may conveniently forget other salespeople who also had high IQs but didn't work out due to lack of motivation, coachability, or some other reason. In short, we "see what we want to see" because it fits our paradigm. Anything outside our own mental paradigm is thus filtered out or discarded.

The vast number of subconscious biases that affect our decision-making abilities would be removed with the use of artificial intelligence during the hiring process. Where AI is considered in this context, candidate data is by construction weighed based on historical evidence and correlative analyses, and not personal preference. The fact is, those aforementioned "mental shortcuts" lead to bad hires with high probability, and that translates to a lot of money lost for companies.

According to CareerBuilder, where total training and opportunity cost are considered, a new salesperson can cost a company a minimum of $45,000. Contrast this with the fact that

[39] "List of cognitive biases." Wikipedia. ttps://en.wikipedia.org/wiki/List_of_cognitive_biases

the predominant weight on a hiring decision is most often given to how an interviewer might perceive a candidate's personality. A question then remains as to whether this makes sense.

In an analysis for the *Harvard Business Review*, Nathan Kuncel discovered that when it comes to evaluating a successful applicant, an algorithm is 25% more accurate in its predictive power. The relevant implication here is that hiring is expensive, and humans aren't all that good at it; hiring for IQ, academic history, extroversion in salespeople, or any of a number of other factors generally held in high esteem doesn't always represent the best criteria. In particular, the way the human mind might predict a great candidate appears far less accurate than the way Machine Learning does it.

For example, simply holding a position open for a high-IQ candidate is likely not a good shortcut to take. According to a study by University of Pennsylvania Professor Angela Duckworth, the best predictor of success among military cadets, teachers, and new salespeople wasn't intelligence but passion and perseverance. IBM conducted an experiment with over 1,000 salespeople and found similar results; goal attainment was positively correlated with "emotional courage" and persistence.[40] In another study by the American Association of Inside Sales Professionals, an AI startup named Koru concluded that experience didn't predict sales success.

There are a myriad of ways that assumption biases can cloud reality. Note this effect holds regardless of whether the job is entry level, in middle management, or in the C-suite.

---

[40] Karsan, Rudy. "With Big Data, Companies Can Predict Your Success Before Your First Day on the Job." *Fast Company*, July 26, 2013.
https://www.fastcompany.com/3014837/with-big-data-companies-can-predict-your-success-before-yo

AI removes many human prediction errors by "automatically mining massive data sets, making predictive inferences of behavior, and predictions around relationships."[41] Furthermore, where there are large numbers of applicants, AI can help process those candidates in a more efficient manner, quickly identifying those who possess requisite skills and are motivated to succeed.

Expanding a bit, artificial intelligence doesn't take the same shortcuts as human interviewers because AI is systematic and logical by construction; it works by considering potentially millions of pieces of data, each of which contributes to a decision on a given candidate. Using algorithmic assessments, statistical models, and patterns from past successful hires, it can search resumes for past experiences or positions and provide insight as to whether those experiences hold any predictive power. Furthermore, as with the other AI-based applications we've discussed, the AI algorithms are "trained" as more data from past hires becomes available.

Let's consider a hypothetical scenario where a sales position at a healthcare software company becomes available. A hiring manager may search his database of resumes for past experience in the healthcare industry, and a list of relevant resumes will become available.

Where the Machine Learning approach differs at this point is that the process is much deeper than a standard Boolean search (i.e., this OR that, this AND that); it can find hidden patterns in data that correlate with success.

For our hypothetical healthcare software company, the algorithm might identify the most successful of those individuals

---

[41] "How Machine Learning Will Shape the Future of Hiring." Riviera Partners. https://rivierapartners.com/how-machine-learning-will-shape-the-future-of-hiring/

that have previously sold other types of products or services in or out of the medical software market. This is a simple thing but still the type of insight that a human might miss due to confirmation bias of what should work (e.g., direct experience in selling similar products) or what seemed to have worked in the past (e.g., high IQ).

Leading edge companies aren't simply using Machine Learning to sift through past experience in resumes; they're also considering the candidate's psychological profile of traits. By analyzing an applicant's psychological profile (or personality) with an algorithm, a lot of subjectivity is taken out of the hiring process. In this case, the psychological profile represents a set of metrics (measures) the algorithm can match via the Machine Learning component with those of your star performers. The mathematics and logic are then quite simple: duplicate attributes of star performers in any new hire and thereby maximize the probability of a successful outcome.

Algorithms can also scour the Internet for important data such as the tone and content of an applicant's social media activity, their LinkedIn profile, and their connections as grist for the mill in narrowing down a pool of applicants.[42] And just to emphasize, the size of the candidate pool isn't a significant factor; this AI is fast, efficient, and completely dogged in performing its task. If there is relevant information to be had, the machine will find it.

In essence, the machine is generating analytics on each candidate to determine capability. For example, relevant capability axes might include an ability to absorb new information (learning), competence (relevant skill-set), organization (logic), communication (writing and speech), and compatibility (values).

---

[42] Alsever, Jennifer. "How AI Is Changing Your Job Hunt." *Fortune,* May 19, 2017. http://fortune.com/2017/05/19/ai-changing-jobs-hiring-recruiting/

The AI Machine Learning algorithms are capable of assessing such attributes to the extent that a manager might realistically expect discovery of a "perfect fit" (should one be present in the hiring pool) relatively early in the hiring process.

Now, one might also expect an unmanageably large number of variables would be required in predicting the success or failure probability of a candidate. In principle, this might be a concern. However, the reality is somewhat different for two reasons: (1) typically not that many variables are required before prediction success is rendered very close to 100%, and (2) anything short of many thousands of such variables are completely manageable for the machine. Such is the power we have at hand this very day.

The basic tool by which this prediction is accomplished is the so-called Artificial Neural Network (ANN). ANN is a digital construct that in some respects models the manner in which neurons in our brain store and process information.

A detailed description of ANN internals is beyond the scope of this work. However, in the most general terms, we can think of an ANN as a massive set of "IF such-and-such is <TRUE/FALSE> THEN this-or-that is <TRUE/FALSE>" statements (productions) reduced to a compact geometric form. Any input we apply fills in those variables present in the IF-THEN statements and accordingly generates an output. Crucially, the training data we've previously applied determines what specific IF-THEN statements are present, and thus the structure of the encoded geometry. As new data is applied, those same statements can be modified, deleted, or expanded depending on whether a given outcome is successful. This is the essence of the Machine Learning process. In simplest terms, the ANN is learning what inputs correspond to a given output.

Finally, if we then regard an input as a "pattern," the output may then be regarded as a classification of that pattern. This is the essence of the pattern recognition capability commonly associated with Machine Learning and also constitutes one form of knowledge representation critical to an AI system. This is also the basis of predictive capabilities associated with AI, whereby inputs are interpreted as a precursor to some expected outcome.

Returning to our example of the salesperson candidate hiring pool, a profile (pattern) for each candidate is applied as input to an ANN trained for this specific purpose. The ANN kernel then processes each input data set and then generates a prediction as to how well a candidate will perform in given areas, or as a whole.[43]

Machine Learning, sans any inherent biases, essentially uses a scorecard much like a human would, but accesses far more data points and typically from many more sources. It weighs each piece of data according to relevance and predictive successes for past employees and then generates predictive analytics.

As has been described, the Machine Learning algorithm is adaptive; it reinforces insights as more data is processed, in principle making each decision and insight more accurate than the previous. As an aside, Machine Learning can also tell when it is not possible to make a high-confidence prediction. This may happen where insufficient data is available, available data is contradictory, or there exists a relationship the AI doesn't understand.

Taking all this one step further, prescriptive analytics takes this information and can advise hiring managers and recruiters on the tangible, quantifiable outcomes of any decision

---

[43] At an even higher level of sophistication, an AI system invoking an entire bank of ANNs will generate ancillary outputs pertaining to confidence intervals, probabilities of success, proposed training schedules, etc.

before it is actually made. Analytics are not just telling you what correlates with success in a role, but also providing directive insights into the best course of action—that is, *whom to hire and why*.

Companies like Clearfit are already creating solutions from new Machine Learning technology in talent acquisition so that the traditional mistakes in hiring aren't made. By providing predictive analytics from the best past hires, technology can now tell you why a certain candidate will be expected to outperform some other seemingly attractive candidate.[44]

Other companies, such as Interviewed, create simulations of what a first day on the job might look like as well as Natural Language Processors (NLP) that measure how articulate and proficient a candidate is in a given language. Algorithms take the diction, tone, and verbiage of successful employees and match the similarities. Measuring a candidate's verbal skills is crucial, especially in a sales position, where customer interaction is compulsory and frequent.

The scope and depth of interviewing candidates are changing dramatically. Hiring managers can now move past standard metrics and use predictive and prescriptive analytics that can help them make smarter decisions, faster.

Large tech companies like Google are leading in the implementation of this new AI technology. In an analysis by the Korn Ferry Institute, Glenn Rifkin writes about Google's transformation in using predictive analytics for hiring:

> At Google, the HR function is called "People Operations," and under Laszlo Bock, the leader of that organization, Google has become the gold standard for hiring analytics.

---

[44] Clearfit. https://www.clearfit.com/

Indeed, all hiring at Google is based on data and analytics and is guided by a "people analytics team." Given its meteoric growth—from its founding just 15 years ago, the company has 45,000 employees and is now the world's second-most-valuable company...

According to John Sullivan, Google's workforce productivity is off the charts. Reportedly, on average, each employee generates nearly $1 million in revenue and $200,000 in profits each year. Google has focused on ways to use data to measure leadership skills, cognitive ability, humility, and ownership.[45]

Just to reemphasize, AI expresses a technological capability to consider and connect massive amounts of data impossible for a human. While the prediction side of hiring is much better off with AI, the final judgment in who is actually hired still goes to a human, and this is the way it should be.

---

[45] Rifkin, Glenn. "Big Data, Predictive Analytics, and Hiring." Korn Ferry Institute. May 12, 2014.

Takeaways:

- Humans are often not good at predicting who is going to be a good hire given inherent biases.

- Hiring the right candidate has become a critical path to a company's ability to generate revenue and survive.

- Machine Learning can use many more data points to find the right candidate with a higher probability of success.

- Machine Learning algorithms get smarter as more historical data on past employees is entered.

# CHAPTER 11

# Lead Prioritization & Engagement

*Like The sales pipeline is the lifeline of any business. "Fix the pipeline, you fix the business" is an often-stated adage. The new wrinkle of our digital age is that while marketing has become so adept at using the latest tools to generate a plethora of new leads, sales personnel find themselves in the blessed and cursed position of trying to keep up as they struggle to qualify, prioritize, follow up, and connect with those numerous leads.*

Anyone who has ever watched David Mamet's 1992 movie *Glengarry Glen Ross* vividly remembers the scene where Blake (played by Alec Baldwin) is sent from the home office of Mitch and Murray to "motivate" the sales team. He then addresses the seemingly over-the-hill sales team about the company's frustration with not enough sales leads being closed.

He shows the team the "Gold Leads" (on red index cards wrapped in string) but refuses to hand them out because they would be wasted on sales guys who can't close the leads they already have. Blake engages Levene (played by Jack Lemmon) and Moss (played by Ed Harris) about their inability to close existing leads. Here's an abbreviated (and uncensored) version of the verbal exchange:

**Blake:** *You got leads. Mitch and Murray paid good money. Get their names to sell them! You can't close the leads you're given, you can't close shit, you ARE shit, hit the bricks pal and beat it 'cause you are going out!*

**Levene:** *The leads are weak.*

**Blake:** *"The leads are weak." Fucking leads are weak? You're weak. I've been in this business fifteen years.*

**Moss:** *What's your name?*

**Blake:** (Addressing Moss) *FUCK YOU, that's my name!! You know why, Mister? 'Cause you drove a Hyundai to get here tonight, I drove a eighty-thousand-dollar BMW. That's my name!! And your name is "you're wanting." And you can't play in a man's game. You can't close them. And you go home and tell your wife your troubles. Because only one thing counts in this life! Get them to sign on the line which is dotted! …*

(Addressing the team) *The money's out there, you pick it up, it's yours. You don't—I have no sympathy for you. You wanna go out on those sits* [one-on-one sit-downs with prospects] *tonight and close, close, it's yours. If not, you're going to be shining my shoes.*

(Taking out a large stack of red index cards tied with a string from his briefcase) *These are the new leads. These are the Glengarry leads. And to you, they're gold. And you don't get them. Why? Because to give them to you is just throwing them away. They're for closers.*

(Putting the gold leads back in his briefcase and closing it) *I'd wish you good luck but you wouldn't know what to do with it if you got it. And to answer your question, pal* (addressing Moss again), *why am I here? I came here because Mitch and Murray asked me to, they asked me for a favor. I said, the REAL favor, follow my advice and fire your fucking ass because a loser is a loser.* (He picks up his briefcase, goes into an inner office)

Decades later, you can see that not much has changed about the demands put on salespeople to close more deals. One could argue that in today's hypercompetitive and commoditized environment, where selling based on differentiation has become nearly impossible, it's tougher than ever to close more deals, more often.

Leads are still being generated through prospecting or purchases by the company. Salespeople are still complaining to marketing that the leads are weak, not qualified, and a waste of time.

As a company struggles to hit its annual revenue numbers, leadership continues to be frustrated with their salesforce not closing enough deals, even after being handed the "gold leads wrapped with a string."

Wouldn't it be ideal if it were possible to send in an agent of change like Blake to drop into a regional office, "motivate" the sales team, and then ride off into the sunset in his shiny BMW leaving in his wake a group of fired-up salespeople? That would be great, but we can all agree that (a) that's an unrealistic scenario,

(b) salespeople would quit at the drop of a hat, and (c) human resources would have a major issue with how the situation was handled. If money was the only motivating force, maybe this approach would have some modicum of success.

Yet studies over the last decade or so have shown us that money is a limited motivator; it will motivate in a particular task and only for a particular time. One need only read *Drive* by Daniel Pink to learn that money not only doesn't incite (or excite) intrinsic motivation, but it may actually reduce motivation.

Nonetheless, the problem of being able to handle the influx of leads continues to be a problem for businesses both large and small. We still have the following issues:

- There are too many leads to reliably follow up on all of them.

- Too many leads fall through the cracks and never get touched.

- Salespeople fail to follow up in a timely matter on hot leads.

- Salespeople use their subjective judgment to decide whether to follow up, which often leads to pursuing a lead with little or no hope of closing.

- Managing these leads, even with the help of a Customer Relation Management (CRM) system, is still a daunting task.

- Salespeople are spending a great deal of their time on non-sales activities (e.g., administrative tasks, follow-up bids, presentation preparation, etc.) or with leads that are either low priority or dead-on-arrival (DOA).

- Salespeople are engaging and wasting their time with clients at a point early in the sales process where the clients are not yet ready to make a buying decision.

- Salespeople face frustration, disappointment, and lack of motivation when the leads they did choose didn't close.

This list of issues are overwhelming to managers, who might then simply throw their hands up and "hope" things will work out. The task of managing a sales team and coaching them on how to prioritize and follow up leads may be easy to do if you have a few salespeople, but you can see how this solution is not scalable when you have 20, 50, or 100 or more salespeople. This is where artificial intelligence can help manage clients and sales pipelines.

Salespeople are excited because with the help of marketing, they can generate more leads into their pipeline than ever before, and from a variety of sources beyond the standard referrals:

- Webinars
- Social Media
- Web Ads
- Website Inquiries
- Downloads from White Papers or Studies
- Online Informational Videos

Yet these sources represent "online" channels that add a certain complexity in gathering and following up on leads. So how does one establish a connection with a buyer or decision maker? What's more, each of these channels attracts a different type of buyer persona, and the salesperson must decide how to actually approach each lead.

For example, if you're in the business-to-consumer (B2C) market, Facebook will be a good social media channel to prospect for new business. But, if you sell a product or service in the Business-to-Business (B2B) market, LinkedIn would be a far better social media channel to use. The point here is that "leads" are one thing, and "leads in a sales pipeline" quite another; sales must first identify the buyer and then tailor an engagement to characteristics of the buyer persona.

The salesperson is under great pressure to effectively engage, qualify, and move online leads through the sales process as quickly as possible. It's a difficult task that will of course grow exponentially with every new lead channel being added.

The salesperson is often tempted to either work the leads in chronological order or simply guess at which leads are more likely to close over another. This is also a time-management issue because the aforementioned "pressure" amounts to an imposed schedule—"so much of this-and-that within a given amount of time." The salesperson is then left guessing how best to prioritize leads under the imposed schedule (time constraint). The result is usually a frustrated salesperson who can't close enough deals, a frustrated client who doesn't get the attention (information) she was seeking, and a frustrated management team who has invested a lot of marketing dollars with little or no Return On Investment.

So what can we do right now? Well, let's look at some of the solutions that have already been implemented to ameliorate this situation. We've already discussed Customer Relationship Management (CRM) applications like Salesforce that have been developed to help salespeople manage their contact databases.

With a CRM, the salesperson cannot only manage his contacts, but also any interactions with the client as she moves through the sales process.

Armed with this tool, salespeople are able to track where they're at in the sales process, what information has been exchanged, what activities have been executed, and any buying decisions that may result. The system also provides reminders about when to follow up with a given client based on previous conversations also tracked by the system.

Salespeople today are fully exercising the power of a CRM to manage their client base, but it doesn't seem to be enough as marketing continues to successfully move more leads into the pipeline. The upshot is that sales needs to make "better decisions faster" as to who will be contacted and when.

Some companies use a scoring system based on an assignment of points in order to prioritize leads. For example, if a lead came from a tradeshow, it may be assigned 5 points out of 10. If the lead came from a requested download (e.g., report or whitepaper) from the company's website, they may be assigned 3 points. Why a 3? In many cases, people who request a report are not as far along in the buying cycle as the person who paid money to go to a tradeshow. If they downloaded the paper and then requested an online demo, they may be assigned 6 points. If the person downloaded the study, requested and completed an online demo, and then met with one of your team members at a tradeshow, the lead might be given an 8.

Each company has its own scoring system and point assignment, and this is most often vaguely based on past experience with buyers. No formal study or analysis is involved; the point system is no more than a relative measure of interest amounting to little more than a qualified "guess."

**Figure 17: Conversica Dashboard**

What salespeople need today is a CRM system that can think with them—one that acts like a second brain with a bit of ESP (Extrasensory Perception). Salespeople need a CRM system that can guide their outreach behavior with these online leads (communication), identify who to call (point of contact), rank the lead (priority), indicate when they should call (timing), and formulate suggestions as to what should be said (engagement). What salespeople need today is a virtual sales assistant in the form of a CRM system that can do all the above and preferably without complaining!

New advances and tools in artificial intelligence are appearing on the market to help salespeople to perform exactly this function. It all comes down to helping the salesperson manage his time and leads better.

As we've previously discussed, a key strength of Machine Learning is that the machine learns with every interaction. And here is yet another application where that capability has already proven most useful. This CRM learns more about the clients as interactions develop; using data points from many sources, it can begin to categorize and prioritize leads. The more information it has access to, the more data points it can call on, the smarter the machine will become.

## Hello VSA

Conversica is a company fully committed to developing an AI Virtual Sales Assistant (VSA) that manages, nurtures, and tracks online leads through the power of artificial intelligence.

Using predictive analytics, natural language processing, and sophisticated Machine Learning algorithms, this VSA will actually reach out to your contacts for you! It will interact with them via email, and they will be none the wiser. When the prospect has been nurtured sufficiently far along in the sales cycle to the point of engagement, the VSA will then hand off the prospect to the salesperson. Think about that for a second! A VSA will interact with your leads on your behalf and only "bother you" when they believe the prospect is nearing a buying decision. Here's what Conversica has to say:

> Conversica provides an automated sales assistant powered by artificial intelligence software. The assistant works just like a human sales assistant, reaching out to every single one of your leads and engaging each of them in a human conversation. People love it because the assistant is personable, friendly, and responsive, connecting them quickly with a human that can help. Salespeople sell more, because the assistant contacts and qualifies all leads so salespeople can focus on what they do best... selling.[46]

---

[46] Conversica. http://www.Conversica.com

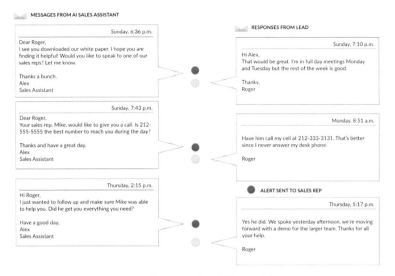

**Figure 18: Conversica VSA Dialogue**

Here's a list of what VSA can already do and how it or something like it will impact your business:

- Free up your salespeople for actual selling by having the VSA sift the qualified leads from the unqualified ones.

- Follow up with every single lead, including inactive leads. With the VSA, you can reach out to clients who haven't bought recently, or who inquired in the past but never bought.

- Gather critical business intelligence such as phone numbers, best times to call, and intent to buy.

- Improve your sales process with a sales assistant who follows up after the salesperson has engaged the client to make sure that he's satisfied with the service (attention) he's receiving.

The benefits of the AI-driven VSA are truly endless. It will open up many possibilities and opportunities to grow your sales revenue in a given market segment or even a saturated market. This amounts to one of those "secret weapons" one simply can't ignore.

Let's drill down a bit. In a given market, the limit to growth may simply be a matter of bandwidth—the ability to touch more clients in a given day. Using a VSA will offload the chore of prioritizing, connecting, and nurturing *all* of your leads.

If on a given day, a salesperson spent 2 hours sifting through leads and doing outreach, that time can now be spent on sales activities that matter most, closing deals for example. Each salesperson will now have an additional 10 hours per week (2 hours saved x 5 days per week) to focus on activities having direct impact on revenue. Of course, every job and task within the salesperson's purview in some sense drives revenue. However, closing sales is where the "rubber hits the road," and incidentally where the human touch is most required.

In a saturated market, the power of an AI-driven VSA will reveal opportunities that would have otherwise gone untapped. Consider the fact that Machine Learning is a pattern recognition machine that can discern patterns in the form of combinations of buying personas impossible for the human mind to perceive.

For example, based on existing information you already have in your database, you can probably come up with 5–10 buyer profiles or personas (i.e., people most likely to buy your product or service). In doing so, you'll use variables found in demographics (e.g., male, female, income level, marital status, etc.), geographic (location, length of time in the home/location) or psychographics (charities, political leanings) to determine who to go after. No problem. You're good. This is how we've been segmenting markets for the last century.

Eventually, you might even reach a limit of how many buying personas are actually present in the market. However, and here's the kicker, the limit isn't in the number of market personas, but in our inability to perceive new variables and their possible connections on which those personas depend. Get ready to accelerate.

**Up and Running Quickly for Rapid ROI**
Your sales assistant arrives for the job fully trained, fully motivated, and already equipped with the experience gained from millions of customer conversations.

FULLY TRAINED — FULLY MOTIVATED — FULLY EXPERIENCED

**Figure 19: Trained and Ready to Serve (Conversica)**

Along comes Machine Learning, which can now use sophisticated algorithms to analyze your current database at a level of detail in terms of content and interconnection simply unavailable to any human agent. It can also be programmed to incorporate other databases with numerous variables, and then, given access to unstructured data (e.g., obtained via social media channels), it can identify seemingly obscure data points, draw deep correlations, and thus build new, far more revealing buying persona profiles.

By obscure data points, I mean it can take an existing buying persona, track its social media activity, and find patterns that we would otherwise miss. For example, a potential client in your database goes online and posts a photograph of a dog along with some mention of a graduation celebration. The Machine Learning algorithm detects a pattern of buying using various data points including the type of pictures people will post and where they're at in their lives (e.g., kids are graduating). Seeing this pattern, the machine prompts the VSA to reach out with a simple, "Congratulations on your Son's Graduation!" or "We here at ABC Company are also dog lovers, and a percentage of all purchases go to the Humane Society." The next thing you know, an inactive lead engages in a conversation with the VSA that eventually leads to the once-inactive client placing her first order. That's the power of using AI to discover new buying personas in an otherwise saturated market. The more data you collect, the more likely you are to discover or uncover markets that are right underneath your non-AI nose.

The algorithm may even be used to generate correlation with obscure data points and find some hidden insight or buying persona. Continuing the example above, in gathering data points from social media (people are dog lovers and their child is graduating), the algorithm may highlight that families with a pet who have a child going to college may have a high level of interest in pet boarding services and vacation excursions in the future. Armed with this new insight, a company can either market its services to this demographic (buying persona) or sell this data (i.e., leverage their data asset) to companies who do sell those services and would be willing to pay for that insight. As we've been saying here, the possibilities are endless. Better yet, let's make that statement more precise: The possibilities for increased profit are endless.

Takeaways:

- Today's salesperson is not capable of prioritizing, managing, engaging, and nurturing the best leads.

- Too much time is wasted on poor leads, and the costs are mounting as marketing continues to drive more and more leads into the pipeline.

- The salesperson is the bottleneck in growing a company's revenue.

- Virtual Sales Assistants can manage and nurture the leads on behalf of the salesperson until the lead is ready to be contacted by the salesperson.

- Machine Learning with VSAs will gain more power in generating predictive market insights and help companies discover new markets and new buying personas.

CHAPTER **12**

# My VSA – Amelia

*Amelia is capable of transformational impact... Allowing her to transform a service desk enables the enterprise to realize savings on average above 60%, while improving customer experience by bringing down the time to resolution of incidents. Extending her reach, in a phased manner, to allow companies to move towards a full digital transformation for competitive gains is a natural derivative of her prowess.*[47]

Chetan Dube, CEO IPsoft

In 1998, Chetan Dube decided to leave New York University, where he was a professor of IT. Fast forward to today, and Chetan Dube is the CEO of IPsoft, an artificial intelligence company that

---

[47] Flinders, Karl. "Chetan Dube: The man behind the robot that will help man extend his horizons." *Computer Weekly*, 2015.

is literally standing on the other side of the AI hype-cycle. He is making believers out of non-believers in the coming age of Machine Learning. He is convinced that machines can and will be used to make business and enterprises more efficient by cloning human intelligence. IPsoft's tagline is "The Digital Labor Company"; this is his clarion call as he leads his company to revolutionize the marketplace via replacement and displacement of human labor with robot labor. We've heard before how AI will change and transform the labor force. The hype around AI has been around for a few decades, but Dube believes that this time it's

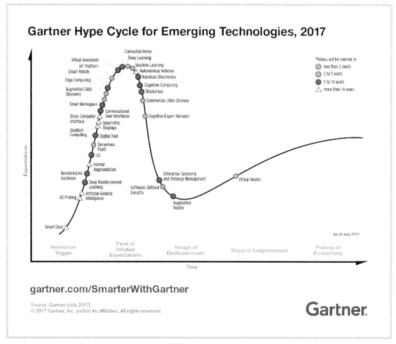

**Figure 20: Gartner Hype Cycle**

for real. On the question of overestimating the short-term effect of technology, Dube says, "AI went through the classic Gartner Hype Cycle of a peak of heightened expectations followed by a trough of disillusionment. This trough of disillusionment led to a period of an 'AI winter,' when there wasn't much research or funding for AI-related domains."[48]

We'll get back to the main topic momentarily, but the "Gartner Hype Cycle" warrants a closer look in order to better understand how technologies touted as "emerging" actually emerge or not. Each hype cycle passes through the five key phases of a technology's life cycle:[49]

1.  **Technology Trigger:** A potential technology breakthrough kicks things off. Early proof-of-concept stories and media interest trigger significant publicity. Often no usable products exist, and commercial viability is unproven.

2.  **Peak of Inflated Expectations:** Early publicity produces a number of success stories—often accompanied by scores of failures. Some companies take action; most don't.

3.  **Trough of Disillusionment:** Interest wanes as experiments and implementations fail to deliver. Producers of the technology shake out or fail. Investment continues only if the surviving providers improve their products to the satisfaction of early adopters.

---

[48] ibid

[49] The hype cycle is a branded graphical presentation developed and used by the American research, advisory, and information technology firm Gartner, for representing the maturity, adoption, and social application of specific technologies. The hype cycle provides a graphical and conceptual presentation of the maturity of emerging technologies through five phases. https://en.wikipedia.org/wiki/Hype_cycle

4.  **Slope of Enlightenment:** More instances of how the technology can benefit the enterprise start to crystallize and become more widely understood. Second- and third-generation products appear from technology providers. More enterprises fund pilots; conservative companies remain cautious.

5.  **Plateau of Productivity:** Mainstream adoption starts to take off. Criteria for assessing provider viability are more clearly defined. The technology's broad market applicability and relevance are clearly paying off.

Now returning to the central point, Dube confesses that past proclamations of AI may have been exaggerated (i.e., "hyped"), and in the end, we've already succumbed to Amara's Law: "We tend to overestimate the effect of a technology in the short run and underestimate the effect in the long run."[50]

Even so, the algorithmic tide of advancement has changed in the last few years with the ability of companies to now aggregate enormous amounts of data to feed into the machines along with the exponential increase in the amount of computer processing power now available to data scientists. Both contributions—Big Data and faster computers—have resulted in the development of increasingly sophisticated algorithms executing in shorter periods of time.

---

[50] Roy Charles Amara was an American researcher, scientist, futurist and president of the Institute for the Future who is best known for coining Amara's law on the effect of technology. "We tend to overestimate the effect of a technology in the short run and underestimate the effect in the long run." This law has been described as encouraging people to think about the long-term effects of technology, and has been described as best illustrated by the hype cycle, characterized by the "peak of inflated expectations" followed by the "trough of disillusionment".

Dube believes that we've arrived at an age where the use of artificial intelligence is not only possible, but scalable to large enterprises. Dube's proof is the introduction, or should I say in the present context, reintroduction of Amelia, IPsoft's Virtual Assistant.

> IPsoft, the digital labor company, has *leapfrogged the current AI market* (emphasis added) by introducing the most comprehensive and human artificial intelligence platform available today, Amelia. The evolution of Amelia connects AI into the very heart of the enterprise and drives value all the way from front office to back office.
>
> With a unique combination of humanlike intelligence and machine powered analytics, Amelia will allow business enterprises to scale customer interactions (i.e., number of conversations) and transform the end to end processes in order to stay ahead of the digital pack.
>
> Multiple breakthroughs in Amelia's cognitive capabilities have drastically advanced her ability to converse with her human counterparts in more than 40 languages in a completely natural, context aware dialogue. In parallel, new analytical capabilities allow her to enrich every user interaction with decisions based on real time data insights.
>
> Together these strengths make Amelia the *only AI* (emphasis added) ready to excel in roles spanning the entire value chain for tomorrow's digital winners. These roles range from servicing customer requests for new insurance policies and assessing risk profiles for new loan applicants to advising employees on HR policies and ensuring supplier billing matches contractual agreements.[51]

---

[51] "IPsoft Introduces the Most Human AI Technology on the Market." Press Release, June 1, 2017.

## Stage 1 - The Virtual Assistant

Amelia is a conversational AI virtual assistant fully capable of interacting on a human-to-human level with clients and can also execute a variety of useful tasks. Amelia uses natural language processing and is able to empathize and respond, adopting the customer's emotional state. Using a set of concepts and categories in the realm of human interaction, Amelia is able to adjust her emotional state with a customer to increase emotional alignment.

Amelia's ability to use a combination of Natural Language Processing, Sentiment Analysis, and Tone Analysis allows her to really hone in on the customer's mood, intent, and attitude. This provides Amelia with a capability to engage one layer below the textual conversation level. Visually, Amelia can also generate facial expressions that will simulate a pseudo-authentic personal experience with each client.

## Amelia Calling

Using a VSA is the preordained future of selling when it comes to lead prioritization and nurturing. The ability of the VSA to further mimic an expert sales assistant and engage the client like an expert salesperson is achievable. The team over at IPsoft believes in this vision. This is a company who has been researching the anterior and posterior neo-cortex functions of the human brain in order to replicate the human mind and insert them into a VSA with an almost eerie level of sophistication, comprehension, intelligence, and human mimicry.

**Figure 21: IPsoft's Amelia, the Virtual Sales Assistant**

Meet Amelia, your personal VSA. Amelia has the ability to store your client database in her virtual mind, but she's much more than just a data repository. Her virtual mind can process information at a speed and scale beyond our own human limitations.

Trainable and coachable, Amelia is able to incorporate the company's sales processes and practices along with the ability to learn more about her clients with every conversation. She also has the capability of understanding client sentiment and can adjust her expressions accordingly.

One of the many hurdles in selling and customer retention is the ability of the sales representative to transmit to the customer that he understands the challenges their business faces. Customers want to know that you (a) understand their business challenges, (b) you are just as concerned as they are, and (c) you are committed to helping them. This is all about empathy, but communicating empathy is actually a complex proposition.

One of the biggest risks a company takes in hiring front-line sales representatives (reps) lies in the fact these individuals will interact with their most valued customers. One wrong word, one misinterpreted expression or statement, and the client may decide to take her business elsewhere. How many deals have been lost because the sales rep didn't answer the client's questions or concerns to her satisfaction? How many clients have been lost to inattention by the sales rep who is handling multiple calls or putting out fires? How many clients have been lost due to a tinge of irritation or impatience in a sales rep's voice?

Questions such as this might well cause a sales manager to panic, but here is where Amelia can help. If the prospect's tone on the call is serious, Amelia's facial expression will adjust to visually transmit that she is concerned as well. If the mood turns light, Amelia will smile. "Amelia understands the underlying meaning of your statements and can engage in fluid conversations. As she detects a customer's mood, she is able to adapt the content of her responses and associated expressions to create a truly personal experience."[52]

Now, with all this capability at hand, Amelia is also programmable and available 24/7/365. Beyond just inserting her into your sales process, where else might you insert her in your company's value chain? Shipping? Customer Service? Accounting? The possibilities are again endless. "Amelia's comprehensive understanding of a company's processes and systems means she can act rapidly to tie conversations with clients, suppliers, and employees together and translate them into a single, streamlined series of actions. The result is straight through processing of optimized decisions."[53]

---

[52] IPsoft. http//www.IPsoft.com
[53] Ibid.

**Figure 22: Inside the Mind of Amelia (IPsoft)**

According to IPsoft, here are six aspects of Amelia's virtual knowledge that enable her to learn, adapt, and execute directives:

- Conversational Intelligence: Human-like natural dialogue is an essential element to working closely with AI.

- Advanced Analytics: Performance analytics and intelligent decisions amplify interactions between human and technology.

- Experience Management: AI and human talent can work together so as to exceed user experience expectations.

- Business Value: New business models are built on the advantages of a digital workforce.

- Supervised Automated Learning: The ability for an AI to naturally learn from Small and Medium Enterprises (SMEs) by observation is key to making businesses dynamic.

| **Case Study:** Leading Nordic bank SEB employs Amelia as an IT Service Desk Agent |
|---|
| SEB, the leading Nordic corporate bank, has completed a rapid deployment of IPsoft's cognitive virtual agent Amelia inside their IT Service Desk. The Amelia pilot rolled out in August 2016 and within three weeks interacted with 700 bank employees and handled 4000 conversations. |
| The project met its targets two weeks ahead of schedule. During the rollout, an SEB project team member commented, "The response is always positive when we introduce Amelia to the staff. As soon as Amelia is demonstrated, the room fills with positive energy." |
| Of her first 4000 conversations the majority were solved by Amelia, so agents were freed from repetitive employee queries. As for the queries Amelia cannot resolve, she observes the employee-agent interaction, learning how to deal with similar variations. |
| Once her learnings are approved by her human supervisors she can answer these queries herself. The pilot phase also measured the ability to automate requests end-to-end by integrating Amelia with IPcenter, IPsoft's service delivery platform. SEB had already deployed IPcenter through a long-standing contract with IPsoft, so new automations were quickly deployed. |
| Amelia integrates securely with SEB back-end systems via IPcenter's autonomic engine, giving her a robust platform to engage with. By adopting Amelia in its IT Service Desk, SEB can |

improve user experience and speed up response for requests, while providing staff with time to dedicate to more complex requests. The bank's deployment highlights the potential of integrating digital labor, autonomics, people, processes and technology into a single system. Amelia's performance has inspired SEB to continue the journey.

The bank is now extending its use of Amelia to incorporate support centers and customer-facing channels. Amelia's role covers two internal business cases which make up 15% of the Service Desk volume: Identity Access Management and Knowledge Management. These were chosen after prioritizing 90 tasks Amelia was capable of supporting. Amelia is engaging directly with employees to:

- Unlock Active Directory accounts
- Unlock accounts for a mortgage application for home loans
- Provide password guidance
- Supply knowledge base answers to questions like "How do I order remote access?"

Source: http://www.ipsoft.com/2016/04/29/amelia-it-service-desk-agent-at-an-european-bank/

Leveraging a VSA that can learn every aspect of your business is mind-boggling and also reassuring.

Amelia's preset inventory comes with common understandings of industry processes. However, all of her modules have self-learning capabilities that enable cultivation of a learning process to specific organizational needs. She constantly improves her performance by updating her knowledge base, via Machine Learning and analysis of all known previous conversations.[54]

One of the challenges many companies and business owners face is training employees on all aspects of the business, only to have them leave for another opportunity elsewhere. Employees leave for many reasons: compensation, mismanagement, upward mobility, relocation, and so on.

Amelia will never leave your company. In fact, she will be with you from the very beginning and grow in expertise just as your business grows. She will learn every aspect of your business and in significant respects, may eventually come to know it better than you. "Amelia utilizes advanced Machine Learning models to make business decisions drawn from conversational data in real-time. She also measures her own business impact across a wide range of metrics and suggests opportunities for improvement."[55]

Add to all this the fact she's loyal by construction, willing to learn, consistent, persistent, never takes a vacation or sick day and, as it stands today, won't complain about the long hours or working overtime.

One could argue that humans have higher Emotional Quotients and will always dominate in this area. For the time being, you are absolutely correct. But the thing humans significantly lack is the ability to efficiently multitask beyond 2 or 3 tasks.

On the other hand, Amelia (an AI platform) can have literally thousands of parallel conversations with customers. At present, Amelia is already perfect for handling conversations that require routine or mundane tasks to be executed. Where those

---

[54] Ibid.

[55] Ibid.

higher-order emotional tasks might be involved, where a client needs to speak with "the manager," those could still be handed off to a human counterpart for resolution.

## Augmented Help

One of the key benefits of using AI to extract actionable insights is the enhancement of the customer's buying experience. This is a big deal because the customer experience will impact bottom-line revenues both long-term and short-term. This Buying Experience differs from customer to customer since each will have their own set of needs and demands. Today's customers want you to:

- Offer unique, valuable perspectives on the market

- Help them navigate alternatives in the marketplace

- Provide ongoing advice and consultation

- Helps them avoid potential "landmines" (e.g., making a buying mistake)

- Educate them on new issues and outcomes

When working with different customers and scenarios, Amelia generates a database of business insights and intelligence from every interaction and every challenge (i.e., "problem" and "resolution"). As we've described, she uses Machine Learning to both access and assess large amounts of data and then generate actionable insights, which allows Amelia to either provide useful suggestions or resolve the client's concerns altogether. This ability to access, assess, and subsequently address problems in "real-time" positions Amelia to resolve many of the anxieties today's customers might experience:

1. Customers are so overwhelmed with the amount of information out in the market that they are literally suffering from information fatigue.

2. Customers need help when it comes to figuring out what will work for their unique situation.

3. With changes in the market (e.g., new product, new regulations, new policies, etc.), it's virtually (no pun intended) impossible for a human to keep up with these changes, let alone make sense of them.

4. Customers see things from their own personal perspective and are isolated from how other customers have handled similar problems or situations. Customers have limited or no access to alternative means to solving problems.

5. Customers sometimes seek domain experts to guide their buying decisions. They want to speak to someone who really knows and has successfully navigated the same or similar experiences. Unfortunately, one of the downsides of the current (furious) evolutionary pace in the marketplace is that finding a "trusted advisor" has become increasingly difficult.

Amelia's ability to use Machine Learning to tap into a reservoir of customer exchanges and problem resolution scenarios gives her an advantage over the human agent when it comes to offering possible solutions.

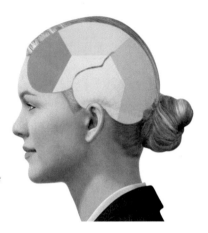

**Experience Management**
She selects the most appropriate response from her multiple knowledge engines to keep the dialogue progressing fluidly. When Amelia needs to escalate a call, she passes on all relevant information to her human colleague so the conversation can continue without forcing customers to repeat themselves.

**Supervised Automated Learning**
Amelia has an expanded inventory of self-learning tools to help her extract data from large documents, making her easier than ever to train. She constantly improves her performance and updates her knowledge base by learning from her human colleagues. All new learnings are reviewed before she can leverage them during live interactions.

A glimpse into Amelia's brain

| Episodic Memory | Neural Ontology | Process Ontology | EQ Ontology |
|---|---|---|---|
| To understand what your customer wants in context, and provide immediate answers | To allow your customers to have a very natural conversation with Amelia | To execute a process for your customer in order to address their needs | To enable Amelia to adapt her responses to your client's emotional state |

**Figure 23: Amelia Brain by IPsoft**

Amelia is not quite ready to fully replace human domain experts or trusted advisors in this capacity, particularly when it comes to complex tasks that require the human touch. However, she is there to augment experts' ability to resolve the client's problems faster and with more options. Imagine having a virtual assistant that you can train for such a purpose who can also progressively learn how to help you better work with customers. Whether it's solving problems via chat, visual interactions, or using Amelia as a "gopher" to find you the information or insight you need to help a client, using this type of technology will generate cost-saving ripples through any organization.

---

### Car Insurance Company – Sales Agent

Customers seeking an online car insurance quote often must fill out numerous forms with dozens of required fields. It is a time-consuming and often frustrating process. One of the US's most popular insurers is poised to improve this experience by deploying Amelia to act as an insurance sales agent.

The goal of the project is to provide the bespoke service and attention customers would get from a personal insurance assistant and provide it at scale to every customer contacting the insurer online.

Amelia will guide prospective clients through the entire process of getting a personalized quote for auto insurance. Once the dialogue has started, Amelia ensures she extracts all the information required in order to feed the company's underwriting decision system. For example, she will ask customers where they live and how many drivers will be

on the policy. Importantly, Amelia will be checking the dialogue to extract information that has already been provided as part of the conversation rather than walking through a painstaking list of questions in a set order.

During the conversation, customers are free to ask Amelia clarifying questions of their own. For example, what is liability insurance? What is a VIN number? Insurance is a highly regulated industry and only licensed brokers can give specific recommendations for insurance policies. However, Amelia can provide generalized guideline information based on statistics. For example, "most people living in your area have chosen this plan."

Amelia further simplifies the interaction for the user by presenting information on screen so that it is easy for them to see the policy being built and a record of which choices they have made so that they can go back and amend these at any time. The overall experience is much more effective and pleasant as Amelia turns the interaction into a conversation rather than an interrogation and ensures the customer is always content about the next step.

Source: IPsoft

In a room of 500 senior business leaders, industry analysts, and media attending the first Digital Workforce Summit to hear how AI is reshaping the workforce, Dube threw down the gauntlet for the future:

> *"Ladies and gentlemen, we are at a seminal moment where a digital Darwinistic curve is unfolding. And you, as leaders in a corporation, are going to decide whether you wish to be on this side of the (lagging) curve or whether you wish to be on the leader's quadrant of the curve."*

Takeaways:

- The age of the Virtual Sales Assistant (VSA) assistant has already arrived.

- A VSA that can sense what the customer or prospect is feeling and adjust the conversation accordingly is a giant step toward sales augmentation.

- Companies that are not leveraging this type of technology will see their profit margins erode as the cost of training continues to increase.

- Your VSA will never "leave."

# EPILOGUE

By James Glenn-Anderson, PhD

Victor was kind enough to let me have the last word on offering a retro and future perspective on AI.

My own perspective on this latest AI revolution might be a bit different than most because I was actually "in" on the one previous. I'd claim this places me in a somewhat unique position of being able to usefully compare. Now, with my having been around for a while, the new people might immediately suspect I'll drop into some form of those "Well, back in my day" or "In the good old days" type reminiscences. Well, no way, good people. Number one, I'm not *that* old. Number two, there is indeed something new here, and I have to say I'm very impressed. We're caught in the midst of a true revolution, and this one caught me completely by surprise.

Part of the reason I like this new AI is practitioners seem to be agreeing with me, and how could I possibly discount anyone that might agree with me? That's simply out of the question, but I should still clarify; this new manifestation of AI technology appears to hinge on something I've long suspected might be important to further advances, that being pattern recognition. Now, pattern recognition was already in the mix as far as AI was concerned, but its application was at that time by and large specific to certain classes of problems, and I was thinking something more of a ubiquitous nature. In order to explain further, I'll have to tell a story.

I've already alluded to the fact my doctoral advisor had given me this seemingly impossible problem to solve. The specific nature of the problem is irrelevant here, but speaking in general terms, the problem was about doing something called *system identification* on a class of mathematical equations used in creating systems dynamics models. These system dynamics models are used for, among other things, simulation of large-scale socio-economic phenomena and constitute what are more commonly known as "World Models." These models are typically of massive scale, potentially incorporating millions of state variables. My problem, the system identification problem, was to sift through whatever information that might be available that might also be applied to a structural definition of such a model. To be more precise, the logic went something like this: "I'm convinced my world-model obeys a given mathematical formalism that gives me a set of equations that look like such-and-such. I know what state variables are involved (and there are lots of them). This determines my dimensionality. The number of (state) variables also determines a set of free parameters in the model, in this case of an order equal to the dimensionality squared. These parameters can be positive, negative, or zero-valued. I also have available a bit of information pertaining to how variables interact with each other, but it's incomplete. Now, given all this, determine what a likely set of values for all model parameters might be, sufficient to a structural definition (system identification)." Get the picture? The dimensionality, which again can be in the millions, is squared! That's a "1" with twelve zeros behind it, people! What do I do with this?!

My life in a nutshell—I truly agonized over this problem. I just saw it as a complete mess and literally for years didn't know what to do with it, and even went off and did another graduate degree while I continued to think about it. Finally, I settled down and looked it square in the eye. I really faced three problems: (1) managing the sheer scale of all possible solutions (problem representation), (2) exploring the space of possible solutions with some modicum of efficiency (search), and (3) determining when I'd actually arrived at a solution (solution state). Now, I had a few mathematics theorems at hand that could help me with "1" and "2." However, contrary to my own expectation that the mathematics would be the most challenging, it was actually Item "3" that proved most difficult. I realized I had a true AI problem in hand. The difficulty was twofold: (1) sparse information (data) pertaining to what a solution would look like, and (2) a multiplicity of data representations—partly numeric, partly relational, and partly qualitative attributes. How was I supposed to combine such data into a single metric or set of metrics that would tell me when I had reached a solution, or serve as an efficient guide to solution-search for that matter?

Suffice to say, I eventually came up with a solution. In this case, I ultimately used a global fuzzy-logic formalism that allowed me to stitch everything together using confidence distributions. However, as I was finishing off my new AI system, I had this idea.

You see, I wasn't quite satisfied with my solution. It worked quite well, all things considered, and I was able to generate the results I needed to write and defend my dissertation. However, I remained uncomfortable with using confidence distributions as

I had. Well, the mathematics of fuzzy logic was just fine, but I still had to a priori assign confidence distributions upfront.

Crudely put, this was a type of guesswork that could be rendered reasonable and defensible, but still left me feeling a bit queasy. On reflection, I realized I was indeed solving the problem as it had been posed. This was valid in the sense that I was using all the information available to me, per the problem definition. However, I intuitively sensed that things could be dramatically improved. Long story short, it all came down to the fact I needed data, lots of it, in order to pin down those "guesstimated" confidences. This was my segue to the concept of Big Data, although I didn't then think of it in those terms. The Internet was young, and as far as I'm aware, the term hadn't yet been coined.

Anyway, I was already aware of Artificial Neural Network (ANN) classifiers. In fact, ANNs were at the time a newfangled gizmo that were all the rage in pattern recognition circles, and I happened to be teaching the theory to engineers at one of the high-technology companies in the area. Having an intimate knowledge of how they worked, I eventually realized ANNs could help me with my own AI research should I decide to take it further. To wit, if I could simply observe the system as a precursor to defining those confidence distributions, I could then effectively eliminate the "guesstimization" factor. More specifically, if I could use ANNs to progressively "learn" a confidence as opposed to any a priori assignment, my system identification would be rendered that much more accurate and efficient.

Well, despite this revelation, I didn't take it further. The primary reason for this was that any use of ANNs in the manner I'd envisioned would take more processing power, and I simply didn't have any to spare. So, I walked away from it. I graduated and immediately began working in domains having nothing to do with AI and really thought very little about the subject for some years afterward.

Fast-forward to the present day, when I find a completely different scenario in full-force.

AI has been reborn, "What is old becomes new again," and at the root of it all is the availability of massively scaled processing power light years beyond what we once had. Add to that the Big Data resource borne of that fledgling Internet I once ignored as not having much to do with science. I was scarily wrong about that. And, what do I find as a primary mechanism for extracting useful information from this Big Data maelstrom but those selfsame ANNs I once couldn't use because they required too much memory and CPU slices on my then-latest-generation, 8088-based PC. I'm also stunned at the present diversity of AI and Machine Learning applications, not to mention associated trends that show no signs whatsoever of abating.

In this book, we've taken a look at just one of those application domains. *Sales Ex Machina* describes how AI has already transformed the selling game in every respect and aspect, and I must say the present reality of the transformation is simply stunning. What's even more amazing is that this transformation continues to accelerate. From my perspective, I see no end to it.

In my own career, I've often interacted with sales and marketing. There was a mutual respect, and together we accomplished great things. I suspect most of my friends in these domains remain unaware of this revolution happening at their doorstep right now, as we speak. I have a message for them: "Take a very close look at this. AI provides a completely new toolset able to enhance sales and marketing processes in every respect, at every point of the sales pipeline.

"Simply put, this technology will help you to achieve levels of performance impossible with the old ways of doing things. This is not fad nor hype. It really works and is already being deployed at an accelerating pace. All the big boys are playing. Enhanced revenues are racking up, and there's a shake-out going on; 'those who do' versus 'those who don't,' and you can guess who's on the winning side.

"Here's the 'hot tip' from a good friend: If breakout success is what you're seeking, this is the way, where the possibilities for your future success are truly endless."

# GLOSSARY

Algorithm: A logic equation for software intended to allow a computer to solve a problem.

Artificial Intelligence (AI): A device that perceives its environment and takes actions that maximize its chance of success toward a goal, typically in visual perception, reasoning, predictions, and decision-making.

Artificial Neural Network (ANN): Computer networks modeled after the functionality and structure of a human brain that allow a computer to process data. Similar to how information is passed from neuron to neuron in the brain, training data is passed from node to node in AI neural networks allowing the computer to process and correlate data.

Association Rule Learning: Rule-based Machine Learning method for discovering patterns or relationships between variables in a large database.

Bayes' Theorem: Describes the probability of an event based on prior knowledge of conditions that might be related to that event. AI might calculate the probability you will buy a certain item based on the last time you bought it, complementary items, and other variables

Big Data: The gathering and storing of large amounts of information for machine analysis. Data can be collected from social media, business and financial transactions, email, and more. The goal of collecting data is to obtain new insights, patterns, or trends. Machine Learning software requires large volumes of data to produce analytics.

Break-Even Point (BEP): The revenue that is required to cover total costs in an investment. Investing in Machine Learning software, research, and implementation in a company can be costly, and when the amount of new sales resulting from that investment matches the investment, the break-even point is met.

Chatbot: A computer program which conducts a conversation via auditory or textual methods. Modern chatbots use artificial intelligence to learn how to communicate with customers, simulating a real customer service representative.

Churn Analysis: The use of predictive analytics to determine which customers are at risk of severing a relationship with the company, and how to prevent it.

Classification: Parsing out useful information from a set of data and grouping it into relevant categories that an algorithm can use for analysis. The data becomes "labeled" into a group. Transactional information from Target can be classified into groups like "clothing," "food," etc.

Cluster Analysis: Organizing data into groups to show relationships between data. If a group of variables is in the same cluster, they are highly correlated. If two variables are in separate clusters, they are not correlated. It is easier for a machine to find underlying patterns in a set of data.

Close Rate: The percentage of qualified leads a salesperson closes on average.

Customer Relation Management (CRM) Software: A program that aggregates customer information in one place to give businesses easy access to data, such as contact data, purchase history, and any previous contact with customer service representatives.

Database: A collection of information that is organized and centrally stored for ease of access and analysis. A company can collect information on customers' buying habits and store them in a database for future analysis.

Data Set: A collection of related sets of information that is composed of separate elements but can be manipulated as a unit by a computer.

Deep Learning (DL): A type of Machine Learning that is based on automatic learning and pattern detection. This type of learning uses Artificial Neural Networks and does not require algorithms to complete specific tasks.

Heuristic: Simple, efficient rules that people often use to form judgments and make decisions. Judging whether someone will be a good employee based on the prestige of their education is a commonly used heuristic in hiring.

Internet of Things (IoT): Physical devices such as computers, phones, vehicles (and anything else that can receive data) that collect and exchange data through the Internet.

Iteration: An update of weights after analyzing a batch of input records. The processing of a single record in a data set to update the neural net model's parameters. Many iterations are required before the machine is exposed to the complete data set.

Lead: A prospective customer who has expressed interest in a product or service.

Lead Scoring: Lead scoring is a methodology used to rank prospects against a scale that represents the perceived value each lead represents to the organization.

Machine Language (ML): The lowest level of programming language that is understood only by computers because it consists only of numbers. Programmers use high-level languages that have translated from machine language into names and commands.

Multivariate Testing: A technique used to test multiple variables. The goal of multivariate testing is to determine which combination of variables performs most successfully.

Natural Language Processing: A field of artificial intelligence that aims to effectively process natural human language from unstructured to structured data. Companies can monitor their social media pages by processing comments and questions with NLP to efficiently discover common sentiments or needs of their consumers.

Node: A basic unit representing a data point that the machine reads as a value or condition.

Outlier: An observation that is distant in value from the majority of observations.

Pattern Recognition: A branch in Machine Learning that focuses on finding pattern-like regularities in data sets. It is often used with supervised learning systems.

Pipeline: A visual representation of where each potential client is in the buying/sales process, beginning from when a prospect shows interest and enters the pipeline, to the end, when a deal is closed.

Predictive Analytics: An algorithmic toolbox to extract information from existing data sets in order to determine patterns and predict future outcomes and trends.

Prospecting: A step in the sales process that involves finding and qualifying potential customers through social media, networking, referrals, or given leads.

Regression Analysis: A set of statistical processes for estimating the relationships among variables.

Retention: The ability for companies to keep its customers over a period of time.

Return On Investment (ROI): A performance measure used to evaluate the efficiency of an investment. ROI measures the amount of return on an investment relative to the investment's cost. Companies use this measure to determine when they will break even on a potential investment.

Rule-Based Programming: A set of "IF-THEN" statements that uses a set of assertions. Rules are programmed to perform an action based on those assertions.

Sales Cycle: A series of phases that is required to sell a product or service. Though every company may have a different sales cycle, it usually begins with initial contact of an interested buyer, meetings, presentations/demos, and ends with the close of a sale.

Sales Funnel: A marketing tool that uses a buying process model to create awareness, interest and purchase of a product. A sales funnel usually starts with a "hook" (free information, book, etc.) and gradually creates interest with each successive page, ultimately leading to a purchase.

Sensors: A device that receives a desired input of information for storage and processing. Sensors are used in many instances, such as home security; a sensor could detect movement when an alarm system is armed.

Sentiment: The intended meaning or feeling behind words and sentences. Algorithms in Natural Language Processing can detect the speaker's sentiment.

Speech Recognition: The ability of a machine or program to identify words and phrases in spoken language and convert them to a machine-readable format.

Statistical Modeling: Mathematically calculated assumptions or predictions based on a given data set.

Structured Data: Information that is structured, labeled, and organized in such a way that it can be easily searched by a simple algorithm or search engine. Data is most commonly labeled as "structured" when it's in a fixed field in a file, such as a spreadsheet.

Supervised Machine Learning: A process that starts with a large set of input and output data. The algorithm then generates a solution in the form of a "map" connecting input and output data. Based on an error feedback mechanism, the algorithm learns how to associate an input with the correct output. Once the algorithm has reached a high degree of accuracy in predicting the output, the learning process is finished. This is called supervised learning because we are in effect "supervising" comparison of a correct answer (output) with the algorithm's generated answer.

Unsupervised Machine Learning: A process that aims to identify hidden, complex patterns using only input data. Unlike with supervised Machine Learning, there is no explicit "training" data set. However, the algorithm itself arbitrates comparison of any generated predictions with actual outcomes and in doing so determines where a corrective "learning" action might be required. Part of this process may involve generation of new internal structure so as to accommodate previously unknown relationships. In effect, unsupervised Machine Learning manifests architectural degrees of freedom for which an internal self-contained logic directs processing to a successful conclusion.

Unstructured data: Alternatively, "unstructured information." This is information that either does not have a predefined data model or is not organized in a predefined manner. Unstructured information is typically text-heavy, but may contain other data such as dates, numbers, and free-form "statements of facts." Unlike structured data, unstructured data would not be found in formatted representations such as those associated with spreadsheets, but rather exists as "free-floating" content on the Internet, including sources such as blog posts, websites, social media content, etc.

To contact Victor Antonio or James Glenn-Anderson, go to
www.SalesExMachina.com